MORE PRAISE FOR
*A HISTORY OF BRITAIN IN 21 WOMEN*

'A timely reminder that the personal is always political, in the past as well as the present . . . From Boadicea to the astronomer Caroline Herschel, after whom a crater on the moon is named, from computing pioneer Ada Lovelace and artist Gwen John to Margaret Thatcher, Jenni Murray chooses twenty-one women who changed the world, and tells their remarkable stories with her own extraordinary wit, passion and piercing insight. She is the perfect guide to a history of Great Britain through the lives of great women – an inspiration that, as she points out, we need as urgently in the twenty-first-century world as we've ever done.'

**Helen Castor**

'I was fascinated by this well-researched, informative and entertaining book. I knew the names of many of the women among its pages, but not their stories and it was wonderful to read about them via Jenni Murray's warm and well-written prose. Entertaining, enjoyable and scholarly.'

**Elizabeth Chadwick, bestselling author of the**
***Eleanor of Aquitaine trilogy***

'I can't think of any more seductive way of learning about the past than meeting its principals as if they were friends in a room. That's the gift that Jenni Murray gives us; a rare gift because these principals are women. If someone in every country were to write a book like this, scholars might finally admit there are two things – history and the past – and they are not the same.'

**Gloria Steinem**

'Jenni Murray has invited us to her feast of extraordinary women: queens, artists, writers, musicians, scientists and activists. All are entertaining, all bring their talents to the table where confident Nancy Astor sits beside retiring Gwen John, and Fanny Burney describes her harrowing mastectomy to the pioneering doctor Elizabeth Garrett Anderson. As incomparable host, Jenni lets her guests display themselves lavishly, telling their own noble or quirky stories while she delicately inserts anecdotes from her own distinguished life – her teenage yearning for the 'gender-quaking' look of Mary Quant, her terror at the idea of interviewing the redoubtable Margaret Thatcher. This is no closed event. The book invites us all to come in. It's a feast you won't want to miss!'

**Janet Todd, Honorary Fellow of Newnham College and former President of Lucy Cavendish College, Cambridge**

'A fresh and very timely way of looking at British history, illuminated by Murray's own incomparable experience in the world of women's stories. Her twenty-one vignettes – of well-known and little-known alike – benefit from the blend of warmth and scepticism that has long marked her own contribution to national life.'

**Sarah Gristwood**

'*A History of Britain in 21 Women* is impossible to put down or ignore. The legendary Jenni Murray opens up the lives of great figures living and long dead. The veteran interviewer's voice is present throughout; probing, challenging but never drowning out her well-chosen subjects. The book is dedicated to the young but offers so much to women and men of all ages.'

**Shami Chakrabarti**

# A
# HISTORY
# OF
# BRITAIN
# IN 21
# WOMEN

*A Personal Selection*

# JENNI
# MURRAY

ONEWORLD

A Oneworld Book

First published by Oneworld Publications, 2016
This paperback edition published 2017
Reprinted 2017

ISBN 978-1-78607-158-3
eISBN 978-1-78074-991-4

Typeset by Hewer Text UK Ltd, Edinburgh
Printed and bound in Great Britain by Clays Ltd, St Ives plc

Oneworld Publications
10 Bloomsbury Street
London WC1B 3SR
England

Stay up to date with the latest books,
special offers, and exclusive content from
Oneworld with our monthly newsletter

Sign up on our website
**oneworld-publications.com**

FSC
www.fsc.org
MIX
Paper from
responsible sources
FSC® C018072

*For all the young people who need to know.*

'In an anti-male era, it's important to remember that men built the planes, fought the wars, laid the railroad tracks, invented the cars, built the hospitals, invented the medicines and sailed the ships that made it all happen.'

Steve Biddulph, *Raising Boys*

'Rubbish!'                                    Jenni Murray

# CONTENTS

# CONTENTS

# INTRODUCTION

It was Thomas Carlyle, circa 1840, who said, 'The history of the world is but the biography of great men', and, as a girl growing up in the 1950s and '60s, his philosophy was pretty much what I was taught and what I believed. Yes, I saw a Queen crowned when I was three years old, but was told she had no real power. Her role was to look lovely, continue the tradition of royal figureheads and be charming.

The movers and shakers, the people who controlled our lives, made political decisions and dictated how our physical and cultural lives should be lived, were men. The role of a woman was to learn how to be a good wife and mother, do the cooking and cleaning, nurture those around her, and have a bit of education so that she would be fit to raise the next generation.

It was education that fed my growing sense that all was not well with the expectations placed on my gender. At a wonderful girls' high school in Barnsley I began to discover that there were women who had influenced history and challenged the assumption that a woman's place was in the home. Some of them came to my notice and inspired me at school.

Trips to London with my parents introduced me to a couple of famous statues of women, although, even today, they are few and far between. University was a bit of a desert – it astounds me still that I could have studied French and Drama for three years without anyone mentioning that Aphra Behn was the first woman to earn her living writing plays, or that Simone de Beauvoir had written every bit as powerfully as her lover, Jean-Paul Sartre.

As I grew older and the women's movement began to uncover more and more women's history and my years on Radio 4's *Woman's Hour* introduced me to others of whom I had never heard, I concluded that Carlyle could not have got it more wrong.

This book contains only a very small selection of the millions of women who have influenced the history of Britain, but they are my choices. They are the women who, from my earliest years until now, have made me realise that there is more to being a woman than making life comfortable for the men around me. I guess the modern cliché is that they were my 'role models', and I shan't apologise for wanting to pass on the lives of such inspiring characters.

There will, inevitably, be some notable omissions. Why, for instance, I was asked, had I left out Marie Stopes, whose book *Married Love* was the first volume of advice on sex and contraception? I'm afraid, despite all the good work she did, I've never been able to excuse her interest in eugenics. Then, only one Queen is featured in the book – Elizabeth I. She's here because I became obsessed with her during my teenage years. She may have been born to her job, but her journey to the throne was long and hard. She followed her half-brother Edward, the unfortunate Lady Jane Grey, her older, childless half-sister Mary, and as the daughter of the dangerous Henry VIII, who tended to send those who displeased him to the scaffold, including her own mother, Elizabeth's childhood and youth could not have been more difficult or risky.

Of course, Queen Victoria presided over the growth of the British Empire and Elizabeth II has kept the Commonwealth together. She is the longest-serving monarch in British history and her energy and fortitude are quite remarkable. I doubt I've ever been more impressed than when I saw her on television, in her ninetieth year, astride her horse, chatting amiably to the groom who accompanied her. She has a good twenty-four years on me and I doubt I'd even be able to mount, let alone stay comfortably on board. I have nothing but admiration for her. Nevertheless, my main interest lies in the women who made their impact not because they inherited their role, but because they fought prejudice and succeeded despite their background and their gender.

In November 2015 it was proposed that feminism should be cut from the Politics A-level syllabus. The suffragette movement was to be squeezed into a section on 'pressure groups'. Only one political thinker, the eighteenth-century feminist Mary Wollstonecraft, was to be mentioned by name. So still, despite the widely held assumption that women in the twenty-first century have achieved complete equality of opportunity with men, the story of the women who, from the earliest times, went before them and struggled to make their way in a male-dominated world was deemed an unnecessary part of the syllabus.

I remember being furious when one of my sons came home with the textbook he'd been given at school for his twentieth-century British History A-level course. 'Mum,' he said, 'I don't think this is right. I can't find any mention of women in this book except half a page on the suffragettes.' OK, he's my son. He grew up with a mother who made sure her boys understood first that housework and childcare are jobs to be shared between everyone who occupies a household – not just the women and girls – and that the women with whom they would spend their adult lives were as likely as them to be lawyers, vets or journalists.

I also taught them – they might argue I rather banged on about it – what a battle women had fought for the right to vote, to get into university, to be doctors, engineers, astronauts, pilots, rocket scientists, artists, composers – all those ambitions enjoyed by boys, which for so long were considered unsuitable for girls. Not every boy or girl gets the chance to learn such things at home, but it is vital that everyone, male or female, is taught that sexism has no place in the times we occupy.

Let's simply set aside Carlyle's hopelessly outdated view and make sure all our children know that the history of the world is the history of great men *and* women. And that the prejudice faced by women, which, frankly, persists despite the ever-growing feminist movement, means that we have always had to work a whole lot harder to make our mark. The twenty-one women in this book rose above the low expectations of their gender and defied anyone who insisted 'a girl can't do that'. Slowly, slowly, over the centuries, they changed the gender landscape for those of us who came after. Fifty-two per cent of the population, holding up the sky, after all!

'They that scorn the tribes and call us
Britain's barbarous populaces,
Did they hear me, would they listen,
did they pity me supplicating?
Shall I heed them in their anguish?
shall I brook to be supplicated?'

Tennyson gives voice to Boadicea

# 1

# Boadicea

## Birth unknown. Died 60/61 CE

I make no apology for sticking with the name Boadicea. It was what I was taught as a child. Although it's become fashionable to refer to her as Boudicca, it seems to me a much less attractive sound. There's long been debate about how to name her correctly. In *Holinshed's Chronicles* of 1577 she is called Voadicia. Spenser, in Book Two of his epic poem *The Faerie Queene* (1590), refers to her as Bonduca. The modern novelist Manda Scott, in her series of novels about the Iceni queen, calls her Breaca nic Graine and emphasises her role within the tribe as a woman who practised magic and divination. I can find no source for Scott's interpretation, but there does seem to be evidence that Boadicea concealed a hare in her garments. She would let it escape to see how it would run. In that way she would make prophecies.

It was in the nineteenth century that Boadicea became the name that was generally accepted, possibly as a mistranslation, dating from the Middle Ages, of Tacitus, the main source of information about her. Tacitus, a Roman historian and contemporaneous recorder of her period, calls her Boudicca, so I guess, strictly speaking, Boudicca is correct.

To me, though, she will always be Boadicea because I was ten years old when I came across her, and she became the first woman to make me realise that the designated future of a girl born in

1950 – to be sweet, domesticated, undemanding and super-feminine – did not necessarily have to be the case.

My parents took me to London for the first time for a week of seeing the sights of the capital. Buckingham Palace, the Houses of Parliament, Westminster Abbey, the National Gallery – we tramped around them all, but I got a little bored by the endless parade of statues which Dad proudly pointed out as 'REALLY IMPORTANT HISTORICAL FIGURES'. There was Nelson, Oliver Cromwell, King Charles I, the Duke of this and that, and then, by the River Thames, on the north-east corner of Westminster Bridge, in the shadow of Big Ben, there appeared something completely different.

*Boadicea and Her Daughters* rose above me as a great revelation. She's driving her carriage. There are lethal blades sticking out from the wheels. Her massive horses are rearing. She's in complete control of them. I knew a bit about horses. My grandfather – a Private at the end of the First World War – had joined up with his mate from the pit who was the farrier who'd taken care of the pit ponies. They went to the Royal Horse Artillery, never saw action as they were called up in 1918 and, as far as I can tell, had spent their entire National Service galloping around London's parks and parade grounds.

When I was two his friend's daughter set up a riding school with pit ponies that came out from the mines when mechanical haulage took over from horsepower. My grandfather instilled his love of the horse in me and I began riding as a tot. Boadicea's horses as portrayed in Thomas Thornycroft's statue were everything I'd ever dreamed about. As, indeed, was she.

She stands there, arms aloft, defiantly holding a spear in her right hand, a piercing glare in her eye, a crown on her head, her daughters behind her, all ready to take on the might of the Roman armies and defend her territory. She is the 'Warrior Queen'. She is the symbol of British resistance against invasion. She's a woman who won't take her humiliation lying down.

The Thornycroft statue was commissioned by Queen Victoria's

consort, Prince Albert, but wasn't finished until 1905, four years after her death and more than forty years after the death of Prince Albert. Boadicea had become a popular historical figure during Victoria's time. Bouda, the root of Boadicea's name, is believed to have meant victory, so there were clear connections between her and Victoria.

Portrayals of the two queens could not have been more different. Victoria's reign was one of industrialisation and expansion of the British Empire. Her nine children married into royal families across the Continent, earning her the name 'the grandmother of Europe', and paintings and statues are of a rather dour, strait-laced and, in her later years, grieving woman.

Boadicea, on the other hand, is, across the generations, shown as a fierce and angry warrior – tall, with flowing, long red hair, bent on revenge for the appalling treatment meted out to her and her daughters by the Romans and with a ruthless determination to retrieve her lands and people from Roman rule.

Queen Victoria's poet laureate, Alfred Lord Tennyson, wrote his poem 'Boädicéa' in 1865 and draws on the sources written by the Roman historian Tacitus, who lived from 51 CE to 117 CE and spent time in Britain during Boadicea's uprising. His father-in-law, Agricola, served in the Roman army under the Governor, Suetonius Paulinus, so his version of the history could well be that of an eyewitness, albeit clearly from a Roman perspective. Tennyson draws on Tacitus' descriptions, but from a patriotically British point of view:

> Far in the East, Boädicéa, standing loftily charioted,
> Mad and maddening all that heard her in her fierce
>     volubility,
> Girt by half the tribes of Britain, near the colony
>     Cámulodúne,
> Yell'd and shriek'd between her daughters o'er a wild
>     confederacy.

'They that scorn the tribes and call us Britain's barbarous
    populaces,
Did they hear me, would they listen, did they pity me
    supplicating?
Shall I heed them in their anguish? shall I brook to be
    supplicated?
Hear Icenian, Catieuchlanian, hear Coritanian,
    Trinobant!
Must their ever-ravening eagle's beak and talon annihilate
    us?
Tear the noble heart of Britain, leave it gorily quivering?
Bark an answer, Britain's raven! bark and blacken
    innumerable,
Blacken round the Roman carrion, make the carcass a
    skeleton,
Kite and kestrel, wolf and wolfkin, from the wilderness,
    wallow in it.
Till the face of Bel be brighten'd, Taranis be propitiated.
Lo their colony half-defended! lo their colony
    Cámulodúne!
There the hordes of Roman robbers mock at a barbarous
    adversary.
There the hive of Roman liars worship a gluttonous
    emperor-idiot.
Such is Rome, and this her deity: hear it, Spirit of
    Cassivëlaún!

Pretty strong stuff! And Boadicea's story, as told by Tacitus and a later
Roman historian, Cassius Dio (150–235 CE), is a truly terrible one. Not
much is known of her early life, indeed her birth date is unrecorded,
but it is generally agreed that she was born into a royal house as a
member of the Iceni tribe, based in the area now known as Norfolk.

In Manda Scott's modern novels based on Boadicea's life, the
Celtic tribe in which her Breaca nic Graine was raised would

have been a largely peaceful environment where men and women enjoyed equal rights. Scott describes her as being taught to be handy with a weapon, as boys and girls would have taken similar roles in the running of the affairs of the tribe and be taught the skills necessary to defend themselves.

Boadicea was married to the King of the Iceni, Prasutagus, and their ownership of their land and wealth was threatened when Emperor Claudius' invasion of Britain brought them into contact with the Romans around 43 CE. A deal was done between Prasutagus and the Roman authorities whereby he would be allowed to control his lands and money, but only with the status of 'Client King'. In his will, according to Tacitus, Prasutagus left half of everything to his wife, Boadicea, and their daughters, and the other half to the Roman Emperor.

This did not sit well with the Romans. Women in Roman society had no rights of ownership or inheritance. They may have left us with straight roads, hot baths and pretty mosaics, but they destroyed a social structure which had been of such importance to the women of the tribes of Britain – equality. When Prasutagus died in 60 CE the Romans refused to honour his will. Boadicea's attempts to claim her rights were viciously denied. Her kingdom was pillaged by Roman troops. Her estates were confiscated. Her two daughters were raped and she was whipped. Her people were evicted from their homes and farms.

At this point the appearance and character of Boadicea came to the notice of Tacitus and, later, of Cassius Dio. Tacitus tells us she was 'tall, with tawny hair hanging down below her waist, a harsh voice and piercing glare'. Dio informs us she was 'possessed of greater intelligence than often belongs in women'. I know . . . Infuriating! Not an uncommon way to describe a powerful, articulate, clever woman, even today.

It was during the absence of the Roman Governor, Suetonius Paulinus, on a campaign in Wales, that Boadicea, fired by fury and revenge for the appalling torture she and her daughters had suffered at the hands of the Romans, began to organise her rebellion. She gathered together her own Iceni tribe and that of the Trinovantes, a tribe based in Essex who had formerly occupied what is now Colchester. Some eighty thousand answered her rallying cry and in 60 CE she was chosen as leader of the rebellion. With a clear strategic advantage, she arranged for her attack to begin when the Romans were at their weakest, as so many of their soldiers were occupied in Wales.

Tacitus reports that she made a speech from her chariot to her own troops, her daughters beside her, in which she claimed not only to be an aristocrat avenging her lost wealth, but an ordinary person avenging her lost freedom, her battered body and the abused chastity of her daughters. She, a woman, was resolved to win or die. If the men, she said, wanted to live in slavery that was their choice.

Dio reports a similar speech, recorded at a much later date, and he adds that the Queen stressed that Britons were a very special people, separated from the rest of humankind by the sea and enjoying, until the Romans came, a liberty unknown elsewhere.

First Colchester was attacked and the archaeological evidence shows that it was methodically demolished. The ninth legion was wiped out. The city was torched and archaeologists have found a thick layer of red soot from the time when Boadicea set the city on fire. The George Hotel in modern Colchester's High Street has a glass pane in the basement revealing a hole that shows the burned red clay.

The rebellion moved on to London, which was then only a small merchant settlement. The rebels burned it to the ground and slaughtered everyone who had not evacuated the city. Evidence of the conflagration again is shown in archaeological research. A thick layer of red dust, similar to the one uncovered in Colchester, coated coins and pottery dating before 60 CE.

St Albans – then Verulamium – was the next Roman settlement to be razed to the ground. Tacitus describes the rebels' choice of location for their attacks as where 'loot was the richest and protection weakest'. He also describes the ferocity of the attacks and the absolute confidence of Boadicea's troops in the justification of their actions and their belief that they would succeed. 'Their confidence was so great that they brought their wives with them, installing them in carts stationed at the edges of the battlefield.' He also claims that more than half the British army were women.

Tacitus details what he describes as the merciless, vengeful cruelty meted out by the Britons. Seventy to eighty thousand Romans were killed, and Tacitus says the Britons were not interested in taking or selling prisoners, only in slaughtering by gibbet, fire or cross. Dio offers even more graphic descriptions of the killings: 'the noblest women were impaled on spikes and had their breasts cut off and sewn to their mouths to the accompaniment of sacrifices, banquets and wanton behaviour'.

Despite Boadicea's superior numbers it was, of course, unlikely that she would be able to defeat a well-regulated and prepared Roman retribution led by Suetonius Paulinus. The two sides are believed to have met somewhere in the Midlands. Paulinus had collected ten thousand troops and lured the Britons into a pitched battle at a battleground of his choosing. The outcome was an easy Roman victory. Tacitus recounts that eighty thousand Britons died, with the loss of only four hundred Roman troops and a small number of wounded.

How Boadicea met her death is hotly disputed by historians. In Tacitus' first history of the period he claims she committed suicide in defeat by taking poison. Dio, in his work written a century later, claims her army numbered two hundred and thirty thousand in total and the outcome of the final battle, far from being a massacre of the Britons, was very close. He says that numerous Britons escaped and were preparing to regroup when the Queen fell ill and died.

Dio writes that 'the Britons mourned her deeply and gave her a costly burial. But, feeling that now at last they were defeated, they scattered to their homes.' Who knows what really happened? The evidence of the burning of Colchester and London is clear, but there's little evidence of the remains of Boadicea's army or of the Warrior Queen herself. Archaeological surveys carried out in 2010 have led to the belief that her defeat took place in Church Stone in Northamptonshire after her army had travelled north of St Albans to meet Roman infantry advancing towards the town.

The only historical writings we have are of Roman origin so, particularly in the case of Tacitus, the eyewitness and relative of one of Paulinus' soldiers, are likely to contain a degree of propaganda. As a national hero Boadicea has been portrayed and written about across the centuries, but the facts are scant.

There's an area on the outskirts of Thetford in Norfolk that archaeologists have found was the capital of the Iceni of East Anglia. The results of the earliest digs on the northern outskirts of the town led to the area being named 'the palace of Boudicca'. It's now called Boudicca's holy place rather than palace, but Thetford's importance in the story of her tribe is clear. The Ancient House Museum at Thetford has a collection of military artefacts described as evidence of the Roman reprisals against her revolt.

Similar, less verifiable, sites exist elsewhere. In the sixteenth century *Holinshed's Chronicles*, a history of Britain, said she was from Northumbria and had burned down Doncaster. There's a chronicle of Scotland that claimed she was from Falkirk. John Fletcher wrote a play called *Bonduca* in 1614 in which he surrounded her with druids (it has been said that Stonehenge was her burial ground) and characterised her as a witch and a most unpleasant woman.

Not everyone has loved or admired her. A British author named Gildas, who wrote in the sixth century, was an aristocrat whose family had benefited from the Roman occupation. He described her as 'a treacherous lioness who butchered the governors who had been left to give fuller voice to the endeavours of Roman rule'. A spot of bias can be assumed in his description.

There are numerous theories about her burial site, taking in Stonehenge, Parliament Hill Fields in London and Gop Hill in Flintshire, where locals claimed to have seen Boadicea's ghost driving her chariot. Perhaps the oddest theory suggests she is buried between platforms 9 and 10 at King's Cross Station. For some time the final battle was thought to have taken place at Battle Bridge at the crossing of the River Fleet near King's Cross. There is no evidence to support such a theory.

Whatever the truth of her demise, there is no doubt that such a woman existed and I'm with Queen Victoria, Prince Albert and the then Prime Minister, Gladstone, who supported the creation of that wonderful Thornycroft statue. Queen Victoria described her predecessor's treatment by the Romans as 'outrageous' and was keen that she should be given a fine memorial. That memorial still stands, but is somewhat overshadowed by the London Eye on the opposite bank of the Thames. Alongside it is a souvenir stall and a fast food stand, so I doubt the hundreds of tourists who gather around her have any idea who she is.

We should honour and show more respect to the woman who reminds us that there was a time in distant history when men and women in Britain had equal rights to property, power and inheritance; where a woman would take up arms against the men who abused her and her daughters, and where men and women would fight alongside each other to defend their rights and their nation.

She was defeated in battle by superior forces, and after her death the Romans occupied Britain for a further 350 years. They erected forts all around the British Isles to keep any other 'barbarians' at bay, but they are reputed to have been a great deal more respectful to Britain's indigenous peoples after their experience of Boadicea's fighting spirit. Nevertheless, I so wish she had won. The relations between British men and women might have been a great deal different if we'd inherited the sexual politics of the Celtic tribes rather than those favoured by the Romans.

'For the face, I grant, I might well
blush to offer, but the mind I shall
never be ashamed to present.'

Elizabeth to her brother Edward VI in 1549

# 2

# Queen Elizabeth I

## 1533–1603

## Reign 1558–1603

Whenever I've been asked to devise a list of historical figures I would choose to be on my 'Top Girls' dinner party table, number one is invariably Queen Elizabeth I. There are so many questions I would like to ask this towering figure who is, I think, generally agreed to be the greatest monarch in the history of Britain.

How did she manage a respectful relationship with the father, Henry VIII, who had had her mother beheaded on the flimsiest evidence of infidelity? How did she manoeuvre her way through a childhood where she was considered illegitimate, under the rule of a father known to be capricious in the bestowal of his favours, and who frequently resorted to the Tower of London and the axe for anyone who displeased him? How did she deal with the shifting religious sensibilities from Catholic to Protestant and back again? What did she make of her half-sister Mary's marriage to the King of Spain, was she in love with Dudley, was she really a virgin, how did she avoid the pressure to marry and produce an heir, and how did she keep her country solvent and at peace for forty-five years?

Elizabeth's birth followed a quite extraordinary amount of turmoil. Henry VIII had been married to Katherine of Aragon for twenty-four years. She was the widow of his older brother, Arthur. With Henry she had produced one surviving daughter, Mary, had one son, Henry, who died when only fifty-two days old and had suffered numerous miscarriages and stillbirths. As Henry became increasingly desperate for a male heir he lit upon Anne Boleyn. She cleverly repudiated his advances, insisting there would be no sex before marriage, and made herself quite irresistible to him.

The divorce from the devout Catholic Queen Katherine and marriage to Anne Boleyn, ably negotiated by one Thomas Cromwell, would lead to England's separation from Rome, the creation of the Church of England and years of plots and general unpleasantness between the Catholics and Protestants within Henry's realm, which would continue through the reigns of Mary and Elizabeth. And, after all that, the infant turned out to be another girl! The Holy Roman Empire's Ambassador, Eustace Chapuys, wrote that the sex of the baby was 'a great disappointment to the King – and to the lady herself'.

Hearing the baby Elizabeth referred to as Princess Elizabeth, her half-sister Mary declared, 'I know of no Princess of England but myself' and she nurtured a jealous hatred of Elizabeth for the rest of her life.

Elizabeth was only three when her mother fell out of Henry's favour. No male heir was forthcoming and the King's attention fell upon Jane Seymour. He and his spies manufactured evidence of Anne's infidelity with a number of young men, including her own brother, and Anne Boleyn was led to the scaffold on 19 May 1536. Both the King's daughters, Mary and Elizabeth, were declared illegitimate, although the stigma of illegitimacy would prove to be something of a fiction as both were named as Henry's heirs in the Succession Act of 1544. Clearly the two girls would be valuable to Henry as he played the royal marriage game. The price of a royal daughter was high when it came to making alliances with other great powers. Mary and Elizabeth were too useful to be cast aside by their father.

Henry's marriage to Jane Seymour quickly produced a male heir, Edward, although his mother died from puerperal fever within a few days of his birth. He would become the first English monarch to be raised a Protestant, but his short reign of only six years was wracked by turmoil and battling protectors. He had taken the throne in 1547 on the death of his father, but in 1553 he fell ill and died at the age of only sixteen. His mother was the only one of Henry VIII's six wives to have been given a state burial, and she lies alongside Henry in St George's Chapel in Windsor Castle.

Elizabeth, an attractive and clever little girl with her father's red hair, was also being raised as a Protestant, although she was never openly passionate about religion. She did, though, lean towards the Protestants as they were the only people who recognised her parents' marriage and accepted her legitimacy. Katherine Champernowne, later Kat Ashley, a servant in the royal household, was appointed as Elizabeth's 'waiting gentlewoman' in 1536. She was a highly educated woman and became Elizabeth's governess, teaching her languages, history, geography and maths. She also taught her the ladylike arts of needlework, embroidery and dancing, and Elizabeth would write warmly of Kat's abilities as a teacher, saying that Kat took 'great labour and pain in bringing of me up in learning and honesty'. Kat became a member of Elizabeth's own household in the 1540s.

When Kat Ashley had taught Elizabeth as much as she could, she acquired as a tutor William Grindal, who had been a favourite pupil of the most renowned educationalist of the period, Roger Ascham. They had been taught at St John's College, Cambridge, known as a leading centre of humanist erudition. Elizabeth was being well prepared for the future she as yet had no notion she would have, but it's clear from a letter she sent to her brother in 1549 that she was only too well aware of the importance of her education and her intelligence. 'For the face, I grant, I might well blush to offer, but the mind I shall never be ashamed to present.'

The young Princess had a distant but affectionate relationship with her father and, when he married his sixth wife, Katherine Parr, he found her to be an ally who shared the intellectual interests of the growing girl. Anne of Cleves had been rejected, divorced, but survived. Catherine Howard was executed for infidelity, but Katherine Parr outlived Henry, who died in 1547 when Elizabeth was only thirteen.

Katherine Parr, an intelligent and educated woman, and now Dowager Queen, took charge of Elizabeth's education, appointing Roger Ascham himself as her tutor in 1548 after the death of Grindal. Ascham said of his pupil, 'Her mind has no womanly weakness, her perseverance is equal to that of a man.'

She enjoyed the same education as that of a Prince, studying rhetoric, classics, philosophy, history and theology. She also liked to have fun, and loved music and dancing, enjoying both for the rest of her long life. She was also fiercely independent. Elizabeth was allowed to run her own household and her own affairs, with William Cecil as her principal secretary and counsellor. He too was a graduate of St John's and would later become her Secretary of State.

Elizabeth's reputation as the Virgin Queen has followed her through history and, I believe, there may have been two reasons for her reluctance to submit to marriage to any man and lose her power and independence.

First, the fate of her mother and the other wives of her father who incurred his displeasure. She was, admittedly, only three years old when her mother was accused of adultery and executed, and there's no evidence to suggest Elizabeth ever had a close relationship with Anne. Nevertheless, the execution of her own mother must have had a profound effect on a growing girl and her acute intelligence must have made her only too well aware that being a woman offered little choice in the direction of one's own future. It could mean marriage for no reason other than political advantage and the danger of being cast aside on the whim of a husband.

Second was an experience she had after her father's death, when she took up residence in the house of his widow, Katherine Parr. In Philippa Gregory's historical novel *The Taming of the Queen*, Katherine had long been madly in love with the Lord Admiral, Thomas Seymour, the younger brother of Edward Seymour, the protector of King Edward VI. The two were married soon after the death of King Henry – some say with indecent haste – but only after Seymour, an ambitious social climber if ever there was one, had first proposed to Elizabeth. He had been rejected. But the evidence suggests that, even if she were averse to marriage, she was attracted to the handsome Seymour. There are reports of 'romps in the bedroom' and on one occasion Katherine Parr is said to have taken part. According to an account written by Kat Ashley, Katherine Parr held Elizabeth down while Seymour 'cut her gown in a hundred pieces'.

Elizabeth was only fourteen when these romps took place and, of course, it was not uncommon in her day for a girl of that age to be married and expected to take a full part in marital relations. But was Elizabeth as happy to be played around with as court gossip of the day suggests? I am rather tempted to go along with the historian David Starkey's analysis of these incidents. He has said that what happened with Seymour would now be regarded as child abuse. My suspicion is that she would have been as horrified by his advances as any modern teenager might be.

Seymour may have been a handsome devil, but I doubt cool, sensible, fiercely independent Elizabeth would have chosen to play around with the husband of her stepmother and protector. Even after Katherine's death in 1548 from puerperal fever, after giving birth to Seymour's daughter, he made another proposal of marriage. Elizabeth again turned down the offer. She was learning from the example of her father and of Seymour that it was perhaps not such a good idea to place yourself in the hands of a man to whom you had to promise love, honour and obedience.

Next came a period in Elizabeth's life that was to prove a further testing introduction to adulthood. Thomas Seymour was caught plotting to replace his brother as protector of their young nephew – during his wild coup attempt he actually shot King Edward's dog. Elizabeth and her closest advisers were suspected of involvement and relentlessly interrogated for weeks. Her servants in the Tower spilled the details of her unsavory relationship with Seymour, but fifteen-year-old Elizabeth refused to incriminate herself: 'This day died a man of much wit and very little judgement' was her cool response to the execution of her stepfather/suitor/abuser.

In 1553 the young King died and his plan to have his cousin, Lady Jane Grey, accede to the throne failed. Mary Tudor became Queen. She immediately repealed all the religious laws of Edward's reign and began to make approaches for reconciliation with Rome. Elizabeth, who the evidence suggests was never a particularly religious individual, outwardly conformed to Mary's Catholicism and she moved to one of her houses – Elizabeth had acquired quite a property portfolio – this time at Ashridge in Hertfordshire.

As Mary's Catholicism was strengthened by her planned marriage to Philip of Spain, she and Elizabeth became increasingly distant and in 1554 Elizabeth was associated with a plot to topple the Catholic regime and put herself in Mary's place. Sir Thomas Wyatt's rebellion failed, Lady Jane Grey and her husband were executed and Elizabeth was taken, yet again, to the Tower, held in the very rooms her mother had occupied before her death.

Elizabeth was questioned by the Privy Council, but again cleverly talked herself out of trouble. The historian John Foxe, in his histories of the Protestant martyrs who had been executed during Mary's reign, counted Elizabeth as one of few to have escaped being burned at the stake as a heretic. He writes of 'The miraculous preservation of the Lady Elizabeth, now Queen of England, from extreme calamity and danger of life'.

She, of course, survived Mary's reign. Philip of Spain had encouraged Mary to reconcile with her sister and to ignore any rumours of her being involved in plots to restore Protestant rule to the country. There's no doubt he would have seen Elizabeth as useful marriage material who would, in the future, help keep England under his control if she were married into a European family of his choice. Elizabeth stayed at Hatfield, another of her properties, and fought off proposals of marriage, while her sister, longing to have a son and heir, went through what was thought to be a pregnancy, turned out to be a phantom pregnancy but may well have been uterine cancer. In 1558 Mary acknowledged Elizabeth as her heir and died eleven days later on 17 November.

And so Elizabeth became Queen, and throughout her rule gave the lie to the ideas put forward in that same year by the Scottish theologian John Knox, who claimed that the 'imbecility of their sex rendered women unfit to bear rule'. Never was there worse timing for a 'First Blast of the Trumpet Against the Monstrous Regiment of Women', the title of Knox's polemic against female monarchs. Elizabeth immediately took full control, appointing her own team of advisers and spies and telling Mary's Privy Council, on the very day of her accession, that she would choose her own council only 'such . . . as in consultation I shall think meet, and shortly appoint'.

By 17 November Cecil was already at the desk he would occupy for the next forty years, and, on 23 November, Elizabeth rode into London for her coronation. No expense was spared – £16,000 was spent – and her popularity with the people was immediately apparent as delighted crowds turned out on the streets of London to welcome their new monarch.

The capital was transformed, in the words of Richard Mulcaster who participated in the pageant, into 'a stage wherein was showed the wonderful spectacle of a noble-hearted princess toward her most loving people and the people's exceeding comfort in beholding so worthy a sovereign and hearing so princelike a voice'. Throughout her reign Elizabeth demonstrated an almost modern understanding of the importance of PR in the way she always presented in public a grand and beautiful image of Gloriana, the Faerie Queene in Spenser's allegorical poem of praise to his monarch. She even at times wore white as the Virgin Queen, appearing to emulate the Virgin Mary.

For forty-five years she reigned alone, relying on clever and devious advisers such as Robert Cecil and Sir Francis Walsingham, and dismissing every attempt to persuade her to marry. The main concern of the men around her, once the religious settlement had been achieved – Protestantism prevailed – was to provide a male consort for the Queen. It was not only Knox who believed a woman was incapable of governing anything more complex than a household.

Even her closest advisers were anxious to present her with a suitable range of suitors, from Robert Dudley, Earl of Leicester, Philip II of Spain, the Habsburg Archduke Charles and the French Duke of Anjou. Their primary objective, of course, was the provision of an heir – a little late perhaps, as Elizabeth was forty-five during her flirtation with Anjou and increasingly unlikely to conceive. The other main worry of her advisers was how a female ruler would be able to fulfil the traditional military role of kings – leading the troops into battle.

Fortunately, she never had to take up arms in person and avoided open warfare in Europe. She attempted to restore the French port of Calais to English control – England had been at war with Scotland and France when she took power and the treasury was exhausted – and then she and the Privy Council skilfully sorted out these matters and the only real threat from a foreign power during her reign came from Spain, when Francis Drake and other privateers incensed the Spanish by successfully plundering their ships. Drake was instrumental in 'singeing the King of Spain's beard', destroying a great deal of enemy shipping in Cádiz, and he brought Spanish treasure worth a staggering £140,000 from the Azores.

On 30 May 1588, 130 ships set sail from Lisbon. The Spanish Armada was intended to prepare an invasion of England, but the outcome was failure for the huge Spanish fleet, largely because the Armada was defeated by terrible weather at sea.

It was in preparation for possible invasion that Elizabeth made one of her best-known appearances. Accompanied by the Earl of Leicester, she visited the camp at Tilbury on the north bank of the Thames. She was in her mid-fifties and had not been well, but she appeared on a white horse, dressed in white velvet with a silver breastplate, and she delivered a phenomenal speech:

Let tyrants fear, I have always so behaved myself, that under God I have placed my chief strength and safeguard in the loyal hearts and goodwill of my subjects. And therefore I am come amongst you as you see at this time not for my recreation and disport, but being resolved in the midst and the heat of battle to live, or die, amongst you all, to lay down for my God, and for my kingdom and for my people, my Honour and my blood even in the dust. I know I have the bodie but of a weak and feeble woman, but I have the heart and stomach of a King and of a King of England too. And think foul scorn that Parma or Spain, or any Prince of Europe should dare invade the borders of my Realm, to which, rather than any dishonour should grow by me, I myself will take up arms.

There is, though, some debate about the authenticity of the speech. Susan Frye, in her article 'The Myth of Elizabeth at Tilbury', says the speech was reported by Dr Leonel Sharp, writing to the Duke of Buckingham in 1623 and he may well have been exaggerating his proximity to the events in Tilbury to inflate his own position as an onlooker at the event.

There is another Tilbury speech, reported by William Leigh in a sermon printed in 1612. It's not nearly so dramatic:

> Come on now my companions at arms, and fellow soldiers, in the field, now for the Lord, for your Queene and for the Kingdom . . . I have been your Prince in Peace, now shall I be in war. The enemy perhaps may challenge my sex for that I am a woman, so may I likewise charge their mould for that they are but men, whose breath is in their nostrils . . . little do I fear their force.

Elizabeth may have delivered both these speeches, or neither, but her presence at Tilbury and her clear talent for public relations – never failing to make herself the centre of England's power – leads me, a self-confessed fan of this extraordinary woman since my schooldays, to believe wholeheartedly that she did deliver the 'weak and feeble woman' version – myth or otherwise. It's a great and inspiring story.

Only one man, Robert Dudley, who claimed to have 'known Elizabeth familierement from before she was eight', might have persuaded the Queen to marry. Court gossip had them in a full-blown affair for a long time, but Dudley was married. After his wife died in mysterious circumstances – possibly murder, possibly suicide – it was assumed the Queen would marry her lover. Soon after, Elizabeth became desperately ill with smallpox and the question of an heir became ever more pressing.

Elizabeth continued to hold out against the idea of marriage, instead ennobling Dudley as first Earl of Leicester. She had thought to marry him off to Mary, Queen of Scots, but Mary married Darnley, like her a great-grandchild of Henry VII. It was a miserable marriage although it produced one son, James, but Mary never escaped the accusation that she had been involved in her husband's murder. Her reputation in Scotland sank further after her marriage to James Hepburn, the Earl of Bothwell. The Protestant lords of Scotland wanted rid of their Catholic Queen. At the age of only twenty-four she was imprisoned, first in Scotland and then in England, for the next nineteen years.

I guess we'll never know whether Elizabeth's alleged affairs, which caused such scandal in the court, ever happened. Rumours of her sexual appetite were even mentioned in a letter to her from Mary, Queen of Scots, warning that her reputation was the subject of much gossip. Maybe she did, maybe she didn't. It is a fact that she left a handsome legacy to the young man who'd been the keeper of her bedroom, so maybe he was rewarded for his discretion. I like to think she did experience some passion with Leicester and Essex, but knew enough not to get pregnant. I doubt she would have wanted the taint of illegitimacy to hang over any child of hers, as it had done in her own case.

Elizabeth's relationship with her Scottish cousin has fascinated me from my teenage years when another tourist visit to London took me to Westminster Abbey. I knew, of course, from history lessons that Elizabeth had had a long correspondence with Mary and had hoped to secure her safely as Queen in Scotland. But Mary had failed in the marriage stakes of which Elizabeth had rightly been so wary. Elizabeth, unlike Mary, never failed to let her head rule her heart and she had no choice but to confine Mary when she came to England seeking asylum from the Scottish lords who had driven her from her own country and placed her son, James VI, on the throne of Scotland.

Mary, as a great-granddaughter of Henry VII, had a claim to the throne of England – arguably stronger than Elizabeth's, given the questions over her legitimacy. Also Mary was a Catholic and inevitably drew support from the Catholic lords in the North of England who would have readily placed her on the throne instead of Elizabeth, thus restoring Catholicism as the national religion.

The two women never met and for years, as plot after plot against her was revealed, Elizabeth refused the solution her advisers pressed upon her: the execution of Mary. Elizabeth believed passionately in the divine right of Kings to rule – a right bestowed upon them by God – and agonised over the decision to remove that right from Mary. It's not difficult to see her logic. If she were to execute a crowned monarch, surely her own position would be put at risk.

Mary's end came in 1586 when the Babington plot was exposed. Anthony Babington was a young Catholic noble who was responsible for passing encoded letters to Mary outlining the plan to murder Elizabeth, release Mary from imprisonment and place her on the throne of England. Elizabeth's superspy, Sir Francis Walsingham, intercepted the correspondence, decoded the letters and presented Elizabeth with the evidence. Mary was found guilty of plotting against the Queen and sentenced to death. Again, Elizabeth hesitated to sign her death warrant – as she had done after an earlier plot involving the Catholic Duke of Norfolk. She refused to sign his warrant three times before he was finally beheaded. Clearly in this aspect she was not her father's daughter!

Mary's death warrant was brought to her among a pile of other papers needing her signature. She later claimed to have signed it to be held in reserve in case of further plots. She said she had not intended it to be sent to Fotheringhay Castle where Mary was held until her execution there on 8 February 1587. Elizabeth is reported to have 'conceived or pretended great grief and anger'. Her strategy seems to have been to blame Burghley and the Privy Council for Mary's death and exonerate herself from the killing of an anointed Queen. Even on her deathbed Elizabeth expressed her regret for Mary's beheading.

It was Elizabeth's tomb in Westminster Abbey that so fascinated me as a teenager. She is buried in the same grave as her sister, Mary Tudor, in the north aisle of Henry VII's chapel in the Abbey. There is no effigy of Mary; Elizabeth's coffin apparently lies above Mary's and the tomb is topped by a rather grand effigy of Elizabeth. There is an inscription in Latin that says, 'Partners both in throne and grave, here rest we two sisters, Elizabeth and Mary, in the hope of one resurrection.' Odd, when they're known to have so disliked each other.

Virtually alongside them, in the south side of the chapel, is the far more impressive tomb of Mary, Queen of Scots. On the wall alongside Mary's grave is a facsimile of the letter sent by James VI of Scotland and I of England – Elizabeth's successor and Mary's son – asking the people of Peterborough to exhume his mother's body and bring her to London where she should be buried with the pomp and circumstance he considered her due: 'That the like honour might be done to the body of his dearest mother and the like monument extant to her that has been done to others and to his dear sister the late Queen Elizabeth.' I was touched by the solicitous nature of a dutiful son, not realising at the time that James was simply writing history to emphasise his own right to his position.

But why is Elizabeth I buried in the same grave as the sister with whom she had nothing in common? Julia M. Walker, in her essay 'Reading the Tombs of Elizabeth I', offers an explanation. Soon after his coronation in 1603, James I undertook a building programme in Westminster Abbey with the aim of reminding his new subjects of his blood claim to the Tudor throne. He was a Stuart, but also a direct descendant of the Tudors through Henry VII.

Elizabeth, at her grand funeral – 'never did the English Nation behold so much black worn as there was at her funeral', wrote the dramatist Thomas Dekker – which took place before James arrived in London, had been buried in the central tomb of Henry

VII, 'in the Sepulchre of her grandfather'. It was the spot Henry VIII had initially planned for his own burial and it was alongside the tomb of her brother Edward VI. James had her moved, reserving that position for himself.

Mary Stuart's tomb is far taller, more imposing and obviously more expensive than that of Elizabeth and Mary Tudor, and the positioning of the graves is highly significant. James planned to place himself in the centre together with Henry VII. Behind Mary Stuart's tomb is the monument to Margaret, Countess of Lennox, James's paternal grandmother. Mary Stuart is also placed in line with Henry VII's mother, Margaret Beaufort. Thus he emphasises the claim of the Queen of Scots to the throne on which Elizabeth sat. He also places her in the line of a dynasty where women bore heirs. Elizabeth and Mary Tudor, both childless, are isolated from the line of women who bore children.

So James I tells us his mother was the unquestionably legitimate great-granddaughter of Henry VII. Elizabeth's legitimacy had been questioned, even by her own father.

I still find it bizarre that Elizabeth I and Mary, Queen of Scots should lie so close to each other in death, given Elizabeth's agony over pronouncing her death sentence and the horrible way Mary died. But I can't agree with James I that Elizabeth should be sidelined as the virgin who neither founded nor furthered the greatness of a dynasty.

James did at least, despite his rather mean-spirited positioning of Elizabeth's resting place, have the decency to bow to convention and have fine words engraved at her head:

### AN ETERNAL MEMORIAL
Unto Elizabeth, Queen of England, France, and Ireland, daughter of Henry VIII, grandchild to Henry VII, great grandchild to King Edward IV. The Mother of this her country, the nurse of religion and learning; for a perfect skill in many languages, for glorious Endowments, as well

of minde as body and for Regal Virtues beyond her Sex A Prince incomparable, James, King of Great Britain, France and Ireland, heir of the virtues and the reign, piously erects this good monument.

Elizabeth held the country together in relative peace for forty-five years and united Scotland and England. She settled the religious upheaval of the previous decades. She gave the generations that followed her an example of courage, education and intelligence, and was my best example as a teenager that John Knox was wrong. We are not a 'monstrous regiment . . . unfit to bear rule', but people of equal abilities when given the chance. We should also bear in mind in the twenty-first century that the production of children is not the only role for which a woman should be valued – monarch or not.

'Who made the laws by which
you judge me? Men!'

*The Rover*

# 3

# Aphra Behn

## 1640?–1689

It still strikes me as quite staggering that I could have spent three years at university studying French and Drama without anyone ever mentioning the first English woman playwright to earn her living by her pen. We studied Shakespeare, of course, and then the fashion for cruel Jacobean revenge tragedies which followed, written by playwrights such as John Webster and Thomas Middleton. Then came the Civil War and the Puritan Interregnum, which saw the execution of Charles I, the exile of his son, Charles II, and no theatre or fun whatsoever under the dour leadership of Oliver Cromwell.

After Cromwell's death in 1658, when young Aphra Behn was about seventeen, the nature of English society began a process of dramatic change. Charles II was asked to return and the monarchy was restored with Charles as King of England, Scotland and Ireland, and the former exile became the 'Merry Monarch'. The theatres were opened again. Women took to the stage for the first time. One of Charles's mistresses, Nell Gwynne, was a talented performer and led the way for other women to follow, and the Restoration comedy became the most popular theatrical genre. At university we studied plays by John Dryden, William Wycherley and William Congreve, the leading dramatists who brought laughter back to the English stage, making fun of the manners of London's newly naughty society.

So my studies were extensive, but strictly male. I really didn't become familiar with Aphra Behn (or Benn as it's sometimes spelled) until the Royal Shakespeare Company, then performing in Stratford and at the Aldwych in London, put on a production of her best-known comedy, *The Rover*, with Jeremy Irons and his wife, Sinéad Cusack, playing the leading roles. It was 1988 and, as soon as I heard the line 'Who made the laws by which you judge me? Men!', I knew I wanted to find out more about her.

Very little is known of Aphra Behn's early life. There are two reliable accounts, according to her biographer, Professor Janet Todd. A Colonel Thomas Colepeper claimed to have known her as a child, writing that her mother was his wet nurse, she was born in Canterbury, her father's name was Johnson and that Aphra was 'a most beautifull woman, and a most Excellent Poet'. Anne Finch, Countess of Winchilsea, is another contemporary commentator who wrote that Aphra was reputed to be 'Daughter to a Barber, who lived formerly at Wye a little market town (now much decayed) in Kent'.

These biographical details match one Eaffrey Johnson, born on 14 December 1640 at Harbledown near Canterbury. She is believed to have been the daughter of Bartholomew Johnson, a Canterbury barber. Her mother, Elizabeth, was from a family engaged in trade, but Elizabeth's brother was an educated man, a doctor trained at Oxford.

It would seem that the playwright John Dryden, England's first Poet Laureate, was right when he wrote after her death that she was lowly born, although her memoir, published in 1698 with her histories and novels, suggests a more elevated background. She describes herself in the memoir, and in her autobiographical portrayal of the central character of her novel *Oroonoko*, as the daughter of a gentleman who 'became the lieutenant-general of six and thirty islands, besides the continent of Surinam'. *Oroonoko* is the story of an African slave taken to the colony of Surinam to serve the English settlers there. There is evidence that Behn wrote her story from personal experience, as she did make a trip to the colony in the early 1660s, and the narrator of the novel is a young Englishwoman clearly based on herself. She gives herself a rather more interesting family history than appears to have been the case.

Todd, in her biography, says of Behn that she 'has a lethal combination of obscurity, secrecy and staginess which makes her an uneasy fit for any narrative, speculative or factual. She is not so much a woman to be unmasked as an unending combination of masks.'

Eaffrey or Aphra had lived her early life during the dull Interregnum – the period between the execution of Charles I in 1649 and the accession of Charles II in 1660 – so she was nearly twenty years old when the Restoration began and saw the revival of the theatre, which had been closed down by the Puritans.

The Restoration comedy was full of handsome rakes, old men seeking a young and vulnerable wife, and fops being ridiculed for their excessive attention to fashion and manners. The plays tended to culminate in a marriage between the rake and the leading lady, which would allow a degree of equality and independence to both.

Bawdy is the term generally applied to the theatre of the period and Aphra would embrace it and form a successful career as a writer, but her sexually explicit work would shock later generations who did not approve of a woman writing about such matters. Thus she rather fell off the radar until the women's movement of the 1970s began to uncover the history of women who had made a mark. Hence, I suspect, her failure to appear on the curriculum of my degree course begun in 1968.

There is, though, an intriguing period of her life that occurred long before she made her name as a writer. During the final years of the Interregnum and the first few years of the reign of Charles II she was employed as a royalist spy. She had somehow met the dramatist and theatre manager Thomas Killigrew, who had spent time in exile with Charles II and was involved in espionage on his behalf. Todd suggests she may have been employed as a copyist for Killigrew because her handwriting was good.

Late in 1663 Aphra arrived in Surinam, the new English colony on the northern coast of South America, administered by a Deputy Governor, William Byam. It was later surrendered to the Dutch. She was accompanied by her mother and siblings, but not her father who is thought to have died before she set out on this mission. She stayed on a plantation owned by Sir Robert Harley and became involved in the politics of the colony. There is evidence that she was acting as a spy as the Deputy Governor's letters refer to her as Astrea – the name she would later adopt as her pen name – and expressed his disapproval of her close relationship with a 'dangerous dissident', William Scot.

William Scot was the son of Thomas Scot, one of the regicides who was executed in 1660 for his role in the signing of the death warrant of Charles I. William had run away to the Netherlands, and Aphra's job, during the Anglo-Dutch wars, which saw England and the Netherlands fighting for supremacy in the North Sea and the Channel, was to befriend him and extract information about the Dutch battle plans.

Behn and her family left Surinam early in 1664. Back in London she married a merchant of German extraction, Johann Behn. The marriage didn't last long. Johann is assumed to have died, leaving Aphra with no means of financial support, so she returned to her spying activities in the Netherlands. In 1666, probably on the instructions of Killigrew and with orders from Lord Arlington, the Secretary of State, she was sent to Antwerp as a government agent under the name Astrea. She was to liaise there with William Scot who was working for the Dutch and try to persuade him to turn double agent. She's thought to have provided some useful information to the government, including a Dutch plot to sail up the Thames and burn the English ships in their harbour.

Aphra found Antwerp a very expensive place to live, so appealed to Killigrew and Arlington for funds, but none were forthcoming. She had to borrow to get herself back to London, but when she found herself unable to repay the debt of £150 she was threatened with debtors' prison. There's no evidence to suggest she was incarcerated, but there's nothing like a need for money to persuade a budding writer to get on with it!

By 1670 she had turned to the stage. *The Forc'd Marriage* or *The Jealous Bridegroom* opened the season of the Duke's Company at Lincoln's Inn Fields on 20 September 1670. It ran for six performances and she was paid the house profits for the third and sixth nights. There's a reference to both her sex and her previous career in the prologue to *The Forc'd Marriage* – 'The Poetess too, they say, has Spies Abroad.'

The play is a tragicomedy dealing with an issue that would not seem out of place even today. Forced marriage – different from an arranged marriage where both parties agree to the union – was made illegal in Britain in 2014, but is known still to take place in some communities. Behn's play tells the story of Erminia who is forced by her father and the King to marry a young warrior, Alcippus, with whom she is not in love. The man she loves and who loves her is Prince Philander, the King's son. Meanwhile, the King's daughter, Galatea, is in love with Alcippus. There is, of course, a happy ending, true love wins and Behn makes quite clear her belief that a woman must have the same choice as any man about where she bestows her sexual favours. The play was considered a success and the following year *The Amorous Prince* was staged. Behn had begun a professional career as a writer for the Duke's Company, under the actor-manager Thomas Betterton.

There had been other women who had written for the stage in the early part of the Restoration, including Katherine Philips and

Frances Boothby, but Behn is extraordinary in her prolific output and the duration of her professional career. The other women had written one or two plays, whereas Behn had at least nineteen plays staged and may well have contributed to many more. Even her earliest works show a total command of the playwright's craft and her subject matter reflects her interest in politics, both state and gender. *The Forc'd Marriage* explores the failure of brute force to achieve a happy union between a man and a woman and celebrates marriage for love. *The Amorous Prince* shows the abuse of power when a Prince uses his position to make sexual demands, and openly tackles fornication and homosexuality.

As a leading light in London's theatrical nightlife, Aphra had a wide circle of friends and is believed to have been the editor of the *Covent Garden Drolery*, a theatrical anthology of verse which included her own work. She also wrote a letter of consolation entitled 'Letter to a Brother of the Pen in Tribulation', which was sent to fellow dramatist Edward Ravenscroft who had been treated for syphilis.

The only liaison she's known to have had since her short marriage, although she wrote affectionately to and about a number of people, was with John Hoyle. He was a bisexual lawyer with a reputation for violence, republicanism and free-thinking, and their names were linked throughout her professional life. There's a reference in a manuscript written in 1687 that 'it was publickly known that Mr Hoyle 10 or 12 yeares since kept Mrs Beane'. She may well have drawn on Hoyle's character for her representations of rakes and libertines, and a series of letters, published after her death as a short story entitled 'Love Letters to a Gentleman', are full of complaints of neglect and appeals for his attention.

Behn became associated with the circle of John Wilmot, the Earl of Rochester, a poet and satirist known for his riotous behaviour in the court of Charles II. He was the perfect example of the

Restoration rake, with a ready wit and a fondness for alcohol and women. He died at the age of only thirty-three as a result of syphilis and alcoholism. It was during Aphra's association with his group that she wrote some of her most risqué poems. They were more openly sexual than any poems published by women at the time and were first attributed to Rochester, only later being correctly credited to her. Her theme was often the pleasure of the woman or her disappointment, and in the best-known, 'The Golden Age', she pleads for a love that is not connected to economic advancement and for sex to be about pleasure rather than power.

Aphra Behn's most famous comedy and the one whose reputation has survived into the twentieth and twenty-first centuries is *The Rover*. It was first performed in 1677 and tells the story of Willmore, a typical Restoration wit who's rather overfond of the drink. He and his friend Belvile take a trip to Naples for 'aimless adventures in pursuit of pleasure'. Behn's female characters dominate and control the action. Hellena falls for Willmore and pursues him disguised as a page, while her sister Florinda sets her cap at Belvile, and both achieve marriages which are demonstrably based on compatibility. The couples are assured financial independence and are not required to demonstrate too much emotional commitment or fidelity. Marriages, indeed, of true minds.

After the sudden death of Charles II in 1685 Behn continued to write for the theatre, but her sexy works became less popular under James II than they had been previously. The last of her comedies was *The Luckey Chance*, published in 1687. Despite her success as a writer of poems and plays she was always short of money and an IOU dated 1685 is for a loan of £6 to be repaid from the proceeds of her next play. That was *The Luckey Chance*, now thought to be one of her best. Its theme is the elderly, lecherous rich man demanding exclusive possession of his young wife. She, of course, is in love with a younger but impecunious man. Her husband's equally repulsive friend procures another young woman as his bride, also in love with a destitute chap of her own age. The young people find a way to be together. True love, again, conquers all and a woman's right to choose her own sexual partners, the theme in so much of her work, is yet again placed centre stage.

Even though the play was a little more morally respectable than some of Aphra's earlier works, tastes had definitely changed and some critics attacked the play as too bawdy and inappropriate for a woman playwright. In her defence, Aphra claimed only to write as men wrote and to be no more or less bawdy than they:

> All I ask, is the Priviledge for my Masculine Part the Poet in me . . . to tread in those successful Paths my Predecessors have so long thriv'd in . . . I value Fame as much as if I had been born a *Hero*; and if you rob me of that, I can retire from the ungrateful World, and scorn its fickle Favours.

Towards the end of 1686 Aphra's often poor health worsened. She was finding it difficult to walk and to write and may have had arthritis. Satirists said it was gout – a condition caused by the excessive consumption of alcohol and rich food – others accused her of suffering from pox and poverty. In 1687 she wrote a letter to a friend in which she said she was 'very ill and had been dying this twelve month'. Nevertheless, Aphra continued to write – she obviously needed the money – and it was during this later period that she produced the novels that seem to have secured her reputation as a writer – arguably the first English novelist: *The Fair Jilt*, *Oroonoko*, *Agnes de Castro* and *The Lucky Mistake*. The first two are now the best known and both draw on her experiences in Surinam and the Netherlands with a female narrator who is clearly based on Behn herself and who observes what occurs around her.

*The Fair Jilt* is about a determined and merciless woman who uses sex to gain power in society, and as a way of dominating men. *Oroonoko* or *The Royal Slave*, her most famous work, has been interpreted as an abolitionist tract and has given Behn the reputation of being an opponent of imperialism and racism. In the last two decades of the twentieth century it became part of the literary canon with numerous editions in paperback.

The story begins with a first-person account of the colony of Surinam and the native people. Oroonoko, a young Prince in what is now assumed to be Ghana, is enslaved and brought to the colony. He is no saint – he has himself been responsible for selling his own people into slavery. He is, though, educated, of a superior social status and, naturally, handsome.

In the final section of the novel Oroonoko leads a rebellion of the black slaves, preferring to die rather than be a slave. He is, one could say, the first example in English literature of 'the noble savage'. His young, pregnant wife is killed and Oroonoko has a particularly grisly end. He is whipped, pepper is poured into his wounds and he dies as a result of dismemberment. The narrator/ Aphra is profoundly disturbed by the events she witnesses, but makes clear that her gender renders her powerless to intervene.

There are a number of other stories worthy of note, particularly a short story called 'History of the Nun', in which a young girl falls into criminal ways because she's been confined too young in a nunnery, and there's a strongly feminist edge to *The Lucky Mistake*, which depicts a young, vulnerable girl with a sharp intellect also caught up in the unwanted attentions of a much older man. It was published posthumously in 1689.

Aphra Behn died on 16 April 1689, only five days after the accession to the throne of William and Mary. She had lived through 'interesting times', but had trodden a largely successful path as a writer through the Interregnum and the reigns of Charles II and James II. Her own epitaph, written 'in her own person', was:

> Let me with *Sappho* and *Orinda* be,
> Oh ever sacred Nymph, adorn'd by thee;
> And give my Verses Immortality.

She was buried in the cloisters in Westminster Abbey and her reputation as a considerable playwright, novelist and poet lasted through the first half of the eighteenth century. A small group of female playwrights acknowledged their debt to her, but as the century progressed women writers were required to write with more 'femininity'. Major authors such as Alexander Pope, Samuel Johnson and Samuel Richardson criticised her for writing like a man and, later in the century, *The Rover* was 'modernised for decency'. In the nineteenth century, according to Professor Todd, she was often described as 'a representative of the culturally disreputable restoration' and as 'a lewd woman whose works, except the redeeming *Oronooko*, should not even be opened'. Julia Kavanagh in her 1863 book, *English Women of Letters*, condemned Behn's 'inveterate coarseness of mind' and said her 'plays were so coarse as to offend even a coarse age'.

The restoration of her reputation as a writer began in the twentieth century when, in 1915, the author and clergyman Montague Summers produced a six-volume edition of her work. She was described by him as a woman who could be placed in the first rank of dramatists. In *Aphra Behn: The Incomparable Astrea*, published in 1927, Vita Sackville-West stressed that Behn was more important as an example of what a woman had been able to achieve than as a literary figure, but it's Virginia Woolf's comment in *A Room of One's Own* that makes Behn such a significant figure for me:

> All women together ought to let flowers fall on the tomb of Aphra Behn, which is most scandalously but rather appropriately, in Westminster Abbey, for it was she who earned them the right to speak their minds.

If you wish to follow Woolf's instruction and let flowers fall, you'll find the grave, not in Poet's Corner, but in the East Cloister with the words 'Here lies a Proof that Wit can never be Defence enough against Mortality.'

'She is very little, very gentle, very modest, and very ingenuous; and her manners are those of a Person unhackneyed and unawed by the World, yet desirous to meet, and to return its smiles.'

Fanny Burney

# 4

# Caroline Herschel

## 1750–1848

You may wonder why a woman such as Caroline Lucretia Herschel deserves a place in a history of *British* women. She was indeed German by birth, born in Hanover on 16 March 1750, but her scientific achievements as an astronomer took place in England. She follows on in her studies of the skies from such feted scientific discoverers as Galileo and Sir Isaac Newton and is a contemporary of Michael Faraday and Edward Jenner. Interestingly, but unsurprisingly, when I, a non-scientist, looked up the timeline for significant scientific discoveries from the fourth century BCE to the present day, she didn't get so much as a mention, but then, guess what, neither did any other woman until Marie Curie in 1898.

Herschel was a great scientist, deserving to be ranked with her famous predecessors. She became the first woman to be paid for her contribution to science, the first to be awarded a Gold Medal of the Royal Astronomical Society and to be named an Honorary Member of the society. That was in 1835 and she took her place together with the Scottish scientist Mary Somerville, of whom more in a later chapter. The Gold Medal, which she won in 1828, was not given to a woman again until the American astronomer Vera Rubin received it in 1996.

She therefore has every right to be here, and as, even today, considerable efforts are required to encourage girls that science is a suitable subject for study for them, the more examples of scientific women who went before the better, in my view!

As has been so often the case with women who have succeeded in their field, it was an attentive father who enabled the young Caroline to receive an education. She was the eighth child and fourth daughter of a mixed marriage. Her father, Isaac Herschel, was a Jewish musician and his wife, Anna Ilse Moritzen, was Christian.

Isaac had served as a bandmaster in the Guards and had been away from the family for long periods before Caroline was born. He became ill after the Battle of Dettingen in 1743 and consequently was at home more frequently after his last little girl was born.

Caroline's prospects were not good when, at the age of ten, she contracted the potentially lethal disease typhus. She was lucky to survive, and indeed to live to the age of ninety-seven, but the illness had a disastrous effect on her growth. She never grew taller than four feet three inches and it was assumed by her parents that such an unattractive little thing would never find a husband. Her father encouraged education, but her illiterate mother insisted she should train to become a housemaid and learn skills such as millinery and dressmaking to enable her to support herself. Her father, during her mother's absences from home, taught her himself and included her in the lessons he gave to her older brother, William.

In 1757, at the age of nineteen, William left Germany for Britain, escaping military service and intending to work as a composer and musician, only developing his interest in astronomy later. He worked as an organist and music teacher at 19 New King Street in Bath, which is now the site of the Herschel Museum of Astronomy.

After the death of their father in 1767, William invited Caroline to come to Bath and live with him, no doubt hoping her training in housewifery would come in handy for him. He agreed to pay an annuity to his mother so that she could hire a new household servant to take Caroline's place. Caroline assumed the aim was to 'make the trial if by his instruction I might not become a useful singer for his winter concerts and oratorios'.

She did indeed learn to sing and, of course, she ran her busy brother's home. She became the principal singer at his concerts and was offered a job in Birmingham, but she refused to work with any conductor other than her brother. She is said to have kept herself very much to the house, except in his company, and to have made few friends.

As William developed his interest in astronomy she again worked at his side, although her memoir suggests a degree of resentment. 'I did nothing for my brother but what a well-trained puppy dog would have done, that is to say, I did what he commanded me.' She does, though, make clear in her writings that she was keen to support herself and have financial independence.

As Caroline became proficient as a singer, taking the leading soprano roles in works such as *Messiah*, *Samson* and *Judas Maccabaeus*, her brother made a dramatic turn in the direction of his career and, consequently, of Caroline's.

He became obsessed with the ambition to explore what he was to call 'the construction of the heavens'. For this he needed the biggest telescopes he could find. He found none that suited his requirements, but he learned how to make his own by visiting the shops of opticians in London. Caroline was expected to do what-ever she could to help in the new venture and she wrote in the summer of 1775 that her time was taken up 'with copying music and practising, besides attendance on my brother when polishing [telescopic mirrors], that by way of keeping him alive, I was even obliged to feed him by putting the vitals by bits into his mouth'.

\*  \*  \*

In 1781 William discovered the planet Uranus while familiarising himself with the brighter stars. His friends in science persuaded King George III to award him a salary which would enable him to give up music and live on the proceeds of his astronomy. The only requirement was that he should show the heavens to the Royal Family when asked. William assumed that Caroline would also give up her career in music to assist in the new venture. She did.

'I found,' she wrote in 1782, after the pair had moved to Datchet, near Windsor, 'I was to be trained for an assistant astronomer; and by way of encouragement a telescope adapted for sweeping . . . was given to me. I was to sweep for comets . . . But it was not till the last two months of the same year before I felt the least encouragement for spending the starlight nights on a grass plot covered by dew or hoar frost without a human being near enough to be within call.'

She endured the discomfort and was rewarded with ever more powerful telescopes, which were more mobile and easier to manipulate. William described one of them thus: 'its movements are so convenient, that the eye remains at rest while the instrument makes a sweep from the horizon to the zenith'.

Caroline and William worked together for some twenty years, producing ever more sophisticated equipment and a number of their most important discoveries of comets and nebulae are directly credited to her. An asteroid was named Lucretia after her middle name and a crater on the moon is called C. Herschel in her honour.

Not only did Caroline gaze at the stars herself, she was also responsible for recording the pair's discoveries. William expected her to record everything, both her discoveries and his. She would sit at a desk in a room near the one where he had set up his telescope and he would shout out the details to her, 'with Flamsteed's Atlas open before her. As he gives her the word, she writes down the declination and right ascension and the other circumstances of the observation.'

She needed the Flamsteed Atlas, drawn up by John Flamsteed,

the first Astronomer Royal, and published in 1712 by Isaac Newton and Edmund Halley, to help her find the star called out by William in order to place the nebulae he needed her to record. She later wrote up a fair copy and carried out the necessary calculations. Her work was published in *Philosophical Transactions* in 1802 by the Royal Society, but in William's name!

Caroline was also responsible for correcting errors in the *British Catalogue of John Flamsteed*, which had remained the standard catalogue of stars of the period. It took her twenty months to assemble a list of the mistakes she and William had found and her list, *Catalogue of Nebulae and Clusters of Stars*, was published by the Royal Society in 1786.

In 1787 she had achieved her ambition of an independent income. She was awarded a royal pension of £50 per annum, making her the first woman to earn her living in science. It wasn't exactly equal pay for work of equal value – William had £200 from the King – but it was a substantial sum, nonetheless.

Caroline was greatly admired by all the professional astronomers of her day, even spending a week in August 1799 at Greenwich with the Astronomer Royal. The novelist Fanny Burney described 'the celebrated comet searcher' as 'very little, very gentle, very modest and very ingenuous; and her manners are those of a Person unhackneyed and unawed by the World, yet desirous to meet, and to return its smiles.'

She had become a respected scientist in her own right, not simply as a helpmeet to her brother, although it seems, as is so often the case for a woman, she was still responsible for all the housework. She lost that role in 1788 when her brother, at the age of forty-nine, married a rich widow, Mary Pitt, and there was, inevitably, some tension in what had been so close and exclusive a relationship between brother and sister.

Caroline destroyed her diaries from that period, and it's often been suggested that she got rid of them because they were full of bitter resentment of the new wife and the brother she had worshipped, but who had pushed her away. I can find no evidence for the suggestion that she became a hostile, jealous spinster. As Burney suggests, her personality was sunny and, while she moved out of the family home to lodgings close by, she returned there on a daily basis to continue her scientific work. She kept up her professional support of her brother, but also pursued projects of her own, making discoveries independently of him. It must have been a relief to get on with her work without having to cook and clean for him!

William was eleven years older than Caroline and in the second decade of the nineteenth century his health began to decline. He died in 1822 and Caroline was so grief-stricken she decided to return to Hanover. There she found she was unable to continue the astronomy which she had pursued with such diligence in England. In her memoir she says, 'at the heavens there is no getting, for the high roofs of the opposite houses'.

She had, though, become very fond of her nephew, John, who had picked up in astronomy where his father had left off. Again, she became an assistant, helping John rearrange their catalogues of nebulae. Sir David Brewster of the Royal Astronomical Society described this work as 'an extraordinary monument of the unextinguished ardour of a lady of seventy-five in the cause of abstract science'.

Herschel had assumed that she was returning to Hanover to die, but she could not have been more wrong. When John visited her in 1832, before he left for the Cape of Good Hope to survey the southern skies, he recorded that his eighty-two-year-old aunt 'runs about the town with me and skips up her two flights of stairs. In the morning till eleven or twelve she is dull and weary, but as the day advances she gains life and is quite "fresh and funny" at ten or eleven p.m. and sings old rhymes, nay, even dances to the great delight of all who see her.'

\* \* \*

# CAROLINE HERSCHEL

Caroline Herschel made her mark in her long lifetime, was eventually recognised as being far more than a mere assistant to her brother and has continued to inspire women who came after her, not only in science, but in poetry and art. Judy Chicago, in her celebrated feminist artwork *The Dinner Party*, made between 1974 and 1979, included Caroline Herschel in her thirty-nine place settings in memory of notable women from history. There is an eye in the centre of the plate, which reminds the viewer of her searches through the telescope. An illuminated capital C cradles a telescope similar to the Newtonian model given to her by her brother. The shape surrounding her name is derived from Herschel's own depiction of the Milky Way. The runner that accompanies the plate is embroidered with images of the cosmos and with concentric rings that point to her work in making charts and maps. *The Dinner Party* is a permanent exhibit at the Brooklyn Museum.

The American poet Adrienne Rich, who died in 2012, was inspired enough by Caroline's achievements to honour her in verse. She began her poem 'Planetarium' with these words:

*Thinking of Caroline Herschel (1750–1848),*
*astronomer, sister of William; and others.*

A woman in the shape of a monster
a monster in the shape of a woman
the skies are full of them

a woman            'in the snow
among the Clocks and instruments
or measuring the ground with poles'

in her 98 years to discover
8 comets

she whom the moon ruled
like us
levitating into the night sky
riding the polished lenses

Galaxies of women, there
doing penance for impetuousness
ribs chilled
in those spaces         of the mind

An eye,
      'virile, precise and absolutely certain'
      from the mad webs of Uranusborg

              encountering the NOVA

every impulse of light exploding
from the core
as life flies out of us

     Tycho whispering at last
     'Let me not seem to have lived in vain'

Caroline Herschel died in Hanover on 9 January 1848 at the age of ninety-seven and was buried there in the churchyard of the Gartengemeinde alongside her parents. The inscription on her tombstone says, 'The eyes of her who is glorified here below turned to the starry heavens.' There was a lock of her brother's hair in her coffin.

'The mother of English fiction.'

Virginia Woolf

# 5

# Fanny Burney

## 1752–1840

Fanny Burney is not the most famous novelist in the canon of English literature, although she was successful and popular in her day. She earns her place in this book because she wrote one of the most courageous and extraordinary pieces of work I have ever encountered. I read it around the time I, like so many other women in twenty-first-century Britain, had been diagnosed with breast cancer.

Burney's is the first example I have come across of a woman writing about so intimate an event as a diagnosis of breast cancer and a mastectomy. It's something we still regard as a rather brave thing to do, but we also acknowledge that it is tremendously helpful to others in a similar position to know that there is no shame attached to the diagnosis; it doesn't have to be referred to in whispered tones as 'the C word', with 'breast' barely getting a mention, and it can be endured and survived. Please, though, bear in mind that in 1811 there was no such thing as an effective anaesthetic! Be brave and read on in memory of Burney and her most supreme courage and will to live.

Burney discovered she had breast cancer in 1810 when she was living in Paris. Her account was written to her sister, Esther, and was entitled 'Account from Paris of a terrible Operation – 1812'.

About August, in the year 1810, I began to be annoyed by a small pain in my breast, which went on augmenting from week to week, yet, being rather heavy than acute, without causing me any uneasiness with respect to consequences: Alas, 'what was the ignorance?' The most sympathising of Partners, however, was more disturbed . . . He pressed me to see some Surgeon . . . Mme de Maisonneuve, my particularly intimate friend, joined with M. d'Arblay to press me to consent to an examination. I thought their fears groundless, and could not make so great a conquest over my repugnance. I relate this false confidence, now, as a warning to my dear Esther – my Sisters and Nieces, should any similar sensations excite similar alarm.

Over the next few weeks she saw a number of doctors – the finest in France, indeed one was obstetrician to Queen Charlotte – but it soon became apparent that they had all agreed that surgery was her only option. She described in detail what happened on the appointed day:

Dr. Moreau instantly entered my room, to see if I were alive. He gave me a wine cordial and went to the Sallon. I rang for my maid and nurses, but, before I could speak to them, my room, without previous message, was entered by 7 men in black. Dr. Larry, M. Dubois, Dr. Moreau, Dr. Aumont, Dr. Ribe and a pupil of Dr. Larry and another of M. Dubois. I was now awakened from my stupor – and by a sort of indignation – Why so many? And without leave? – But I could not utter a syllable.

M. Dubois acted as Commander in Chief. Dr. Larry kept out of sight; M. Dubois ordered a Bed stead into the middle of the room. Astonished, I turned to Dr. Larry who had promised that an Arm Chair would suffice, but he hung his head and would not look at me. Two old mattrasses M. Dubois then demanded, and an old sheet. I now began to tremble violently . . . These arranged to his liking, he desired me to mount the Bed stead. I stood suspended, for a moment, whether I should not abruptly escape – I looked at the door, the windows – I felt desperate – but it was only for a moment, my reason then took command, and my fears and feelings struggled vainly against it . . .

I was compelled . . . to submit to taking off my long robe de Chambre, which I had meant to retain. Ah, then, how did I think of My Sisters! – not one, at so dreadful an instant, at hand to protect – adjust – guard me . . . how did I long – long for my Esther – my Charlotte!

. . . I saw even M Dubois grow agitated, while Dr. Larry kept always aloof yet a glance showed me he was pale as ashes. I knew not, positively, then, the immediate danger, but everything convinced me danger was hovering about me, and that this experiment could alone save me from its jaws. I mounted, therefore, unbidden, the Bed stead – and M. Dubois placed me upon the Mattrass, and spread a cambric handkerchief upon my face.

It was transparent, however, and I saw, through it, that the Bed stead was instantly surrounded by the 7 men and my nurse. I refused to be held; but when, Bright through the cambric, I saw the glitter of polished Steel – I closed my Eyes. I would not trust to convulsive fear the sight of the terrible incision. A silence the most profound ensued, which lasted for some minutes, during which, I imagine, they took their orders by signs, and made their examination – Oh! What a horrible suspension! – I did not breathe – and M. Dubois tried vainly to find any pulse. This pause, at length was broken by Dr. Larry, who in a voice of solemn melancholy, said '*Qui me tiendra ce sein?*' [Who will hold this breast for me?]

No one answered, at least not verbally; but this aroused me from my passively submissive state, for I feared they imagined the whole breast infected – feared it too justly – for, again through the Cambric, I saw the hand of M. Dubois held up, while his forefinger first described a straight line from top to bottom of the breast, secondly a Cross, and thirdly a circle; intimating that the Whole was to be taken off. Excited by this idea, I started up, threw off my veil, and, in answer to his demand, '*Qui me tiendra ce sein?*' cried, '*C'est moi, Monsieur!*' [I will, Sir!] and I held My hand under it and explained the nature of my sufferings, which all sprang from one point, though they darted into every part. I was heard attentively, but in utter silence, and M. Dubois then re-placed me as before, and, as before, spread my veil over my face. How vain, alas, my representation! Immediately again I saw the fatal finger describe the Cross – and the circle – Hopeless, then, desperate and self-given up, I closed once more my Eyes, relinquishing all watching, all resistance, all interference and sadly resolute to be wholly resigned.

My dearest Esther – and all my dears to whom she communicates this doleful ditty, will rejoice to hear that this resolution once taken, was firmly adhered to, in defiance of a terror that surpasses all description, and the most torturing pain. Yet – when the dreadful steel was plunged into the breast – cutting through veins – arteries – flesh – nerves – I needed no injunctions not to restrain my cries. I began a scream that lasted unintermittingly during the whole time of the incision – and I almost marvel that it rings not in my Ears still! so excruciating was the agony.

When the wound was made, and the instrument was with-drawn, the pain seemed undiminished, for the air that suddenly rushed into those delicate parts felt like a mass of minute but sharp and forked poniards, that were tearing at the edges of the wound – but when again I felt the instru-ment – describing a curve – cutting against the grain, if I may so say, while the flesh resisted in a manner so forcible as to oppose and tire the hand of the operator, who was forced to change from the right to the left – then, indeed, I thought I must have expired.

I attempted no more to open my Eyes – they felt as if hermetically shut, and so firmly closed, that the Eyelids seemed indented into the Cheeks. The Instrument this second time withdrawn, I concluded the operation over. Oh no! presently the terrible cutting was renewed – and worse than ever, to separate the bottom, the foundation of this dreadful gland from the parts to which it adhered – Again all description would be baffled – yet again all was not over. Dr. Larry rested but his own hand, and – Oh Heaven! – I then felt the Knife rackling against the breast bone – scraping it! – This performed, while I yet remained in utterly speechless torture, I heard the Voice of M. Larry – (all others guarded a dead silence) in a tone nearly tragic, desire every one present to pronounce if anything more remained to be done; or if he thought the operation complete. The general voice was Yes – but the finger of M. Dubois – which I literally *felt* elevated over the wound, though I saw nothing, and though he touched nothing, so indescribably sensitive was the spot – pointed to some further requisition – and again began the scraping! – and, after this, Dr. Moreau thought he discerned a peccant attom [fragments of diseased breast tissue] – and still, and still, M. Dubois demanded attom after attom – My dearest

Esther, not for days, not for Weeks, but for Months I could not speak of this terrible business without nearly again going through it! . . . I was sick, I was disordered by a single question – even now, 9 months after it is over, I have a head ache from going on with the account! and this miserable account, which I began 3 Months ago, at least, I dare not revise, nor read, the recollection is still so painful.

To conclude, the evil was so profound, the case so delicate, and the precautions necessary for preventing a return so numerous, that the operation, including the treatment and the dressing, lasted 20 minutes! a time, for sufferings so acute, that was hardly supportable – However, I bore it with all the courage I could exert, and never moved, nor stopt them, nor resisted, nor remonstrated, nor spoke – except once or twice, during the dressings, to say '*Ah Messieurs! que je vous plains!*' [Ah, sirs, how I pity you!] for indeed I was sensible to the feeling concern with which they all saw what I endured, though my speech was principally – very principally meant for Dr. Larry. Except this I uttered not a syllable, save, when so often they re-commenced, calling out '*Avertissez moi, Messieurs! avertissez moi!*' [Warn me, Sirs! Warn me!] Twice, I believe, I fainted; at least, I have two total chasms in my memory of this transaction, that impede my tying together what passed.

When all was done, and they lifted me up that I might be put to bed, my strength was so totally annihilated, that I was obliged to be carried, and could not even sustain my hands and arms, which hung as if I had been lifeless; while my face, as the Nurse has told me, was utterly colourless. This removal made me open my Eyes – and I then saw my good Dr. Larry, pale nearly as myself, his face streaked with blood, its expression depicting grief, apprehension, and almost horrour.

There was, of course, a happy conclusion to this terrible story. Fanny Burney was fifty-nine – a fairly typical age for breast cancer to show itself – when she had the mastectomy. She lived, almost, until the age of eighty-eight – another twenty-nine years – and there's clear evidence that a great deal about the treatment of the disease was learned by the medical profession as a result of her successful surgery.

Frances Burney – always known as Fanny – was born in King's Lynn in Norfolk; she was the third child of Charles, who was a musician and author, and his wife, Esther, who was also a musician. Their eldest daughter, Esther, the recipient of the 'mastectomy letter', was born in 1749, rather shockingly for a couple of their time and class, some time before their marriage. A son, James, followed and then came Fanny, who was known in the family, from the age of about eleven, as 'the old lady'. She had, apparently, a rather serious air about her. Three more siblings survived – Susan, Charles and Charlotte – and they became a close-knit family.

Fanny was educated at home, suffered badly from short-sightedness and, according to her father's memoirs, she was 'wholly unnoticed in the nursery for any talent or quickness of mind'. She didn't know her letters at the age of eight, was roundly teased for it by her brother, but developed a passion for literature thanks to her sister. She learned as a result of hearing Esther as she recited passages from Pope 'many years before I read them myself'.

By the age of ten, though, she had mastered the English language and wrote her first novel. It was called *The History of Catherine Evelyn*, but it no longer exists, possibly burned on her fifteenth birthday along with other works and most probably at the insistence of her stepmother. Her mother had died of consumption in 1762, not long after the family had moved to London and set up home in Poland Street in Soho.

Her father became a music teacher and, despite the family's grief at the loss of their mother, they made famous and influential friends, including Samuel Johnson and the actor David Garrick. Fanny continued her writing, experimenting with different literary styles. She and her siblings seem to have got on well with the stepsisters and stepbrother brought to the family by Elizabeth Allen, a widow the Burneys had known in King's Lynn, but the relationship with her was strained. Fanny was a prolific letter writer and kept her diary faithfully throughout her life, in which she was never less than frank when describing her family and the people she met socially. She was not impressed by her stepmother, recording that she and her siblings regarded Elizabeth as 'moody, neurotic and insecure'.

As her father, Charles Burney, became ever more successful as a musician, the family was able to move up the housing ladder. Charles was an organist, composer and the most respected historian of music of his time. He travelled around Europe researching and performing and his final appointment was as organist at Chelsea Hospital from 1783. His *General History of Music*, published in four volumes between 1776 and 1789, and written with the help of his daughter, contributed to a growing fashion for ancient music in late eighteenth-century London and encouraged an appreciation of contemporary work. He was a champion of Handel, Haydn, Bach and Mozart.

Fanny found their home on the south side of Queen Square in Bloomsbury 'a charming house with a delightful prospect'. In that period there had been no urban development to the north and she could see Hampstead and Highgate from her window.

In 1774 they moved up the ladder again as her father gained more prestige from his musical performances, this time to a house built in the 1690s for Sir Isaac Newton in St Martin's Street near Leicester Square. Sir Joshua Reynolds was a neighbour and it was at a dinner at his house that Fanny's father met a wealthy brewer, Henry Thrale. Fanny became a part of the Thrales's social circle and mixed regularly with Dr Johnson and other great literary, artistic and musical figures of the day, including the

'Bluestocking group' headed by Elizabeth Montagu and Hannah More. To be described as a 'bluestocking' was no compliment. It was fashionable to wear fine black silk stockings. Thick, blue worsted stockings were cheaper than silk and only thought suitable for day wear. They were considered practical but inelegant. So, a bluestocking was a derisory term for a woman of intellect who cared more about the quality of her mind than fashion.

Fanny's diaries paint a fantastic picture of the late-eighteenth-century social scene. In one she recounts an entertainment by the Italian singer Gabriel Piozzi, in which she describes Mrs Thrale mocking the performer behind his back. Thrale later married him, and the story would form the inspiration for Virginia Woolf's essay 'Dr Burney's Evening Party'.

The diaries are full of intimate portraits of the man with whom she seems, from her writings, to have had a love–hate relationship – the ageing essayist and lexicographer Samuel Johnson. In 1778 she records:

Monday Sept 21: I have had a thousand delightful conversations with Dr. Johnson who, whether he loves me or not, I am sure seems to have some opinion of my discretion, for he speaks of all this house to me with unbounded confidence, neither diminishing faults, nor exaggerating praise.

Whenever he is below stairs he keeps me prisoner, for he does not like I should quit the room a moment; if I rise he constantly calls out 'Don't you go, little Burney!'

On another occasion, Saturday 2 November 1782, she writes of an invitation to Lady Shelley's house in which Dr Johnson had not been included:

He is almost constantly omitted, either from too much respect or too much fear. I am sorry for it, as he hates being

67

alone, and as, though he scolds the others, he is well enough satisfied himself, and having given vent to all his own occasional anger or ill-humour, he is ready to begin again, and is never aware that those who have so been 'downed' by him can never much covet so triumphant a visitor.

Two days later she was invited with her family to breakfast with Lady De Ferrars, and this time Dr Johnson was included.

I happened to be standing by Dr. Johnson when all the ladies came in . . . but, as I dread him before strangers, from the staring attention he attracts both for himself and all with whom he talks, I endeavoured to change my ground. However, he kept prating a sort of comical nonsense that detained me some minutes whether I would or not; but when we were all taking places at the breakfast table I made another effort to escape. It proved vain; he drew his chair next to mine, and went rattling on in a humorous sort of comparison he was drawing of himself to me – not one word of which could I enjoy, or can I remember, from the hurry I was in to get out of his way.

It's clear she had a much more intimate relationship with him than the one he had with his biographer, James Boswell. In fact, when Boswell – she often refers to him in her diaries as Bozzy – was writing his biography, he begged Fanny for help, asking if he could have copies of Johnson's letters to her, saying, 'I want to show him in a new light. Grave Sam, and great Sam, and solemn Sam, and learned Sam – all these he has appeared over and over. Now I want to entwine a wreath of the graces across his brow; I want to show him as gay Sam, agreeable Sam, pleasant Sam; so you must help me with some of his beautiful billets to yourself.'

Fanny disliked Boswell, describing him as pushy. She refused him access to the correspondence, and her diary records her first meeting with Bozzy at Mrs Thrale's house in Streatham around the time of the publication of her novel, *Evelina*.

> Of everyone else, when in that presence, he was unobservant, if not contemptuous. In truth, when he met with Dr Johnson, he commonly forebore even answering anything that was said . . . lest he should miss the smallest sound from that voice to which he paid such exclusive, though merited, homage. But the moment that voice burst forth, the attention which it excited in Mr Boswell amounted almost to pain.

Fanny's family never escaped having their lives revealed in her diaries, even when the events were considered scandalous. Two of her stepsisters eloped to the Continent, which Fanny at first found rather romantic, but then began to consider shameless and shocking. Then in 1777 her younger brother Charles was sent down from Cambridge when he was caught stealing books from the university library. Frances would later tell Charles's son, after his father's death, that he had had 'a MAD RAGE for possessing a library' and in his later years Charles had indeed amassed a wonderful collection of books and newspapers, many of which are now held in the British Library. What is more likely is that Charles had stolen the books to sell them in London and pay off the debts he had incurred drinking and gambling. The close family came together to hush things up in society, but Fanny was never one to leave anything out of her letters and diaries. Maybe she never intended them for publication.

The impact of her brother's behaviour on Fanny meant that her first novel, *Evelina*, was published in 'extreme secrecy' so as not to draw attention to the family name. The book – with no name attached and using a non-existent Mr King as intermediary – was rejected by the first publisher, James Dodsley. A second attempt was made by Charles who, around Christmas 1776, took the first instalments of the novel to the Fleet Street bookseller Thomas Lowndes, 'in the dark of the evening', muffled up 'in an old great coat, and a large old hat, to give him a somewhat antique as well as vulgar disguise'. Lowndes agreed to publish and offered Fanny twenty guineas in payment. She accepted.

*Evelina* was published anonymously, became very popular and was well received in the *London Review* and the *Monthly Review*. The literary circles in which the Burneys moved soon became aware of the novel. Johnson was fulsome in his praise of *Evelina* after he'd borrowed a copy of the book and said it was more interesting and enjoyable than anything written by either of the popular novelists Samuel Richardson or Henry Fielding.

Sir Joshua Reynolds was reported by Mrs Thrale to have been 'fed while reading the little work, refusing to quit it at table and Edmund Burke sat up all night to finish it'. Booksellers and the fashionable spas were said to be unable to keep up with demand – it was a publishing sensation. But the name of the author was kept a secret until the Reverend George Huddesford published a satirical poem called 'Warley'.

> Poetasters I hold it a sin to encourage,
> Let a pump or a horse pond supply them with porridge.
> Will your scurrilous dogg'rel a dinner ensure ye,
> Or the fee-simple pay of your Manor of Drury?
> Will your metre a council engage or Attorney,
> Or gain approbation from dear little Burney*?

The asterisk guided the reader to a footnote which explained that she was 'The Authoress of Evelina', destroying the complex subterfuge she and the family had employed to keep her authorship hidden. Fanny was furious and wrote in her diary about a dinner party in the company of Sir Joshua Reynolds and Lord Palmerston (the second Lord Palmerston, whose son was to become Prime Minister) where the poem was discussed. She was, she said, 'frightened woefully, felt in such a twitter' and suffered 'infinite frettation'.

*Evelina*, the Cinderella story of a kind of orphan later revealed as an heiress, is a pretty archetypal tale, but it distinguishes itself in its social commentary. It was written in the form of letters and took the reader through the popular resorts of the period in London and Bristol; the characterisation was compelling and it was funny – it was particularly scathing about the vulgar nouveau riche.

Her second novel, *Cecilia: Memoirs of an Heiress*, proved equally successful and the first edition of two thousand copies sold out immediately. It showed a rather unflattering picture of life in high society, again with a humorous edge, and Cecilia's guardians, the snobbish Mr Delvile and his proud wife, were popular characters. Edmund Burke, Edward Gibbon and Johnson all declared themselves fans, with Burke complimenting her on her writing and declaring 'this is now the age for women'.

She'd been paid £250 for the rights by the publisher, around £34,000 in today's money, and was now comfortably off in her own right. In 1784, when Samuel Johnson died, she lost one of her closest and most supportive friends, but that same year she was befriended by Mary Delany, a writer and artist who had been a close friend of Jonathan Swift in the early part of the century and had become a great favourite at court.

Fanny was presented to the King and Queen and was offered the job of second keeper of the robes to Queen Charlotte with a salary of £200 a year and a footman and maid. She was reluctant to accept the offer, writing in a letter to Esther in June 1786, 'The separation from all my friends and connections is so cruel to me – the attendance, dress, confinement, are to be so unremitting.' Her father, though, ever the social climber, urged her to accept. Her relations with her stepmother had worsened, her siblings were married, her close circle of friends was diminishing as they

71

aged and died off, and an unmarried woman in her mid-thirties didn't have a lot of choices. She took the job.

Her journals chronicle five years of servitude ruled by rigid protocol under her immediate superior, Madame Elizabeth Schwellenberg, who she found to be a carbon copy of her step-mother: 'gloomy, dark, suspicious, rude, reproachful'.

She was, though, in the perfect position to witness at first hand the madness of George III. His first serious attack took place in 1788 and her sense of humour creeps into her diary as she describes him in a variety of comical and pathetic situations, one of which involves him chasing her around Kew Gardens. The King's illness increased the stress of her position and she eventually managed to escape after asking the Queen to release her on the grounds of ill health. She retired from the Queen's service on half pay in July 1791.

Fanny returned to the literary world, and in 1793, the year of the execution of the French King Louis XVI, she met a group of French émigrés including Charles Maurice Talleyrand, Mme Germaine de Staël and one Alexandre-Jean-Baptiste Piochard d'Arblay. He was a career soldier who, together with the rest of his aristocratic group, had fallen foul of the Jacobins. They were, though, constitutional reformers, not royalists, and Fanny was attracted to their liberal politics. She avoided friendship with Mme de Staël despite her admiration for her intellect, as she disapproved of her promiscuity. She disliked the sly Talleyrand, but was attracted to d'Arblay. Reader, she married him. She was forty-one and their marriage proved to be extremely happy. They had one child, a son, Alex, who was born in 1794, seventeen months after their wedding.

Fanny resumed her career as a writer, publishing *Camilla: A Picture of Youth* in 1796. She was paid £1,000 for the rights and when a subscription campaign was mounted, leading figures flocked to subscribe at a guinea and a half for the three volumes.

One of the less-exalted subscribers was an unknown twenty-year-old woman called Jane Austen, who publicly announced for the first time that she was a disciple of Fanny Burney's. The novel was not her most popular, but it portrays the kind of difficulties faced by a woman in achieving an education – writers on a similar theme, such as Mary Wollstonecraft, were her contemporaries.

There were difficult years for the d'Arblays at the start of the new century as they travelled between Britain and France during extremely uncertain times. Fanny wrote a number of plays, none of which were performed on the London stage, and it wasn't until 1814 that she published her last novel, *The Wanderer* or *Female Difficulties*. Yet again, a female writer was bringing powerful sexual politics into her fiction as she described what it was like to be a penniless spinster pushed this way and that. She was, though, not short of money by now and was paid £1,500 for the first edition.

Fanny's final years were marked by bereavement. Her brother died in 1817 and her husband in 1818, followed by her sisters in 1832 and 1838, while in 1837, her son, Alex, died of a sudden fever. She herself died in London on 6 January 1840 and was buried at St Swithin's in Bath alongside Alex.

Her fame as a writer increased after her death as her journals, with their vivid portrayals of late-Georgian England and post-revolutionary France, were published. In the first half of the twentieth century Virginia Woolf demanded Burney be admired as a novelist and called her 'the mother of English fiction'. A memorial window was unveiled in Poets' Corner in Westminster Abbey in 2002 by her great-great-great-great-nephew, Charles Burney.

So, despite that ghastly operation, which will, frankly, stay in my mind, and probably yours, forever, Fanny Burney outlived everyone she had loved, including her child. I love her writings, her gossip, her vivid portrayals of life among the London literati of the eighteenth and nineteenth centuries. Most of all I love her for making us all aware that, though the diagnosis is horrific and the surgery (even with a full anaesthetic) isn't pleasant, breast cancer can be survived and a long and extremely productive life lived after it.

'I do not want them to have power over men,
but over themselves . . . It is not empire, but
equality and friendship which women want.'

Mary Wollstonecraft

# 6

# Mary Wollstonecraft

## 1759–1797

I own a lot of books. If there were a fire in my house, only one would be among the few things that must be saved. Three dogs, a cat, a picture of my family and Mary Wollstonecraft's *A Vindication of the Rights of Woman*. It cost me a ridiculous amount of money and it is not even a first edition. Mine was published in 1796, four years after the first, published in 1792, became a runaway bestseller.

The most precious thing I've ever held in my hands, wearing white gloves in the old Women's Library when it was housed at the London Metropolitan University in the East End, was one of the rare surviving first editions of this first, truly great feminist manifesto. It's now held in the library at the London School of Economics.

I'm not generally given to a passion for 'things', but holding these books, even my inferior third edition, excites me more than I ever thought possible. They seem to give me a direct connection to a woman who, far ahead of her time, dared to write down just about everything I've ever believed about what used to be assumed was a woman's only lot and, at times, still is. She often seems quite critical of her fellow females, railing at them for being obsessed with romance, clothes and being pretty and pleasing to men. She describes them as 'teeming with capricious fantasies' and says in *A Vindication* that 'all women are to be levelled, by meekness and docility, into one character of yielding softness and gentle compliance'.

In her most critical passage she declares:

> women's giddy minds have only one fixed preoccupation: the desire of establishing themselves . . . by marriage. And this desire making mere animals of them, when they marry they act as such children may be expected to act – they dress, they paint, and nickname God's creatures. Surely these weak beings are only fit for a seraglio!

She describes marrying for money and security as legal prostitution, but then again she understands the degree to which women are forced into such positions, generally having no rights to an education equal to that enjoyed by boys and rarely an opportunity to earn a living and be financially independent. She does not, in the end, blame women for their own downfall, although she does urge them to drag themselves from the position in which they've been placed. She emphasises that it is not nature but culture that renders women 'weak and wretched'.

'There must,' she writes, 'be more equality established in society, or morality will never gain ground, and this virtuous equality will not rest firmly even when founded on a rock, if one half of mankind be chained to its bottom by fate, for they will be continually undermining it through ignorance or pride.'

Women in the late eighteenth century could assume no rights. Marriage was, for most of them, the best career that could be expected, especially if a husband with a decent amount of money could be found. Once married there was no right for a woman to own a share in property or be protected from domestic violence, and, should a marriage end, the father, not the mother, would be given custody of any children.

There was no right to vote or hold any political office and it was not until 1929 that a case known as the Persons Case, taken by five Canadian women, persuaded the Privy Council in London to agree that a woman should be defined in law as a person. This had not applied in English law before 1929, even though a limited right to vote had been passed by Parliament in 1918 and full suffrage in 1928. It was the Canadian women who won us the right to be defined, like men, as persons. Wollstonecraft's theory that women are made not born would later be echoed by Simone de Beauvoir in *The Second Sex*, published as late as 1949.

Unsurprisingly Wollstonecraft's views were not widely welcomed in her time. Why would men, accustomed to taking a wife as a housemaid, nanny, social secretary and decorative companion, unused to making demands for herself, want things to change? Horace Walpole, the writer, politician and son of the former Prime Minister Sir Robert Walpole, called her 'a hyena in petticoats'.

The second most precious possession on my bookshelves is a first edition, described as 'a new edition', of a book mistakenly entitled *The Rights of Women* – the original was decidedly singular, *Woman*. It was published a hundred years after the original, in 1891, and the introduction was written by one Mrs Henry Fawcett. We now know her rather more correctly as Millicent Garrett Fawcett, one of the leading activists in the suffragist movement (more of her later in the book).

It is clear from Fawcett's glowing approval of Wollstonecraft that her *Vindication* has survived and influenced subsequent generations. Fawcett writes:

Mary Wollstonecraft was ahead of her time and may be regarded, though opinion has moved in the direction in which she pointed, as ahead of ours. In numerous passages she points out the inseparable connection between male and female chastity. One would have thought the fact so self-evident as to need no asseveration; but as a matter of experience we know that even now the mass of people mete out to the two partners in the same action an entirely different degree of blame, and judge them by entirely different standards . . . Against the essential immorality and injustice of this doctrine and practice Mary Wollstonecraft protested with her whole strength. She exposes the insincerity of those who profess zeal for virtue by pointing the finger of scorn at the woman who has transgressed, while her partner who may have tempted her by money, ease, and flattery to her doom, is received with every mark of consideration and respect.

Fawcett goes on:

In one other important respect Mary Wollstonecraft was ahead of her own time in regard to women and in line with the foremost thinkers on this subject in ours. Henrik Ibsen has taken the lead among the moderns in teaching that women have a duty to themselves as well as to their parents, husbands and children, and that truth and freedom are needed for the growth of true womanliness as well as of true manliness . . .

I have already quoted her saying: 'I do not want them to have power over men, but over themselves' . . . 'It is not empire, but equality and friendship which women want' . . . 'Speaking of women at large. *Their first duty is to themselves as rational creatures*' . . . The words italicised foreshadow almost verbatim Nora's expression in the well-known scene in 'A Doll's House', where she tells her astounded husband that she has discovered that she has duties to herself as well as to him and to their children . . . Women need education, need economic independence, need political enfranchisement, need social equality and friendship . . . That woman must choose between being a slave and a queen; 'quickly scorn'd when not ador'd' is a theory of pinchbeck and tinsel . . . Upon this theory, and all that hangs upon it, Mary Wollstonecraft made the first systematic and concentrated attack; and the women's rights movement in England and America owes as much to her as modern Political Economy owes to her famous contemporary, Adam Smith.

Margaret Walters, in her biography of Wollstonecraft, suggests that like the heroine of her first novel (*Mary: A Fiction*, published in 1788), who rejects her parents, Wollstonecraft had 'no models, no one to identify with, so she ha[d], literally to invent herself'. Walters points to the fact that Mary faced the barriers experienced by all women who are determined to exercise their independent minds and suggests it is this all too familiar struggle which gives such a 'curiously modern' quality to her story and explains why we still identify with her so strongly today.

Like so many women who managed to make their way and fulfil 'their first duty to themselves as rational creatures', it was Mary's father who lit what we would now call her feminist light bulb, although in her case, not in a good way. Her family life is a prime example of how the personal becomes political.

She was born in Spitalfields in London in 1759 into a relatively prosperous family. Her paternal grandfather owned a successful silk-weaving business, and when he died in 1765, her father inherited a share of the concern.

With no experience or knowledge of farming he moved his wife and children to live on a farm in Epping in Essex. Edward Wollstonecraft senior failed at every business he attempted and his daughter Mary would later describe him as a childish bully who abused his wife and family after heavy drinking sessions. She would often intervene to protect her mother from his violence. Elizabeth, her mother, seems to have made no protest on her own behalf.

There were seven Wollstonecraft children – Ned, Mary, Henry Woodstock, Eliza, Everina, James and Charles – and Ned was undoubtedly his mother's favourite. Mary would later write in her novel *Maria: The Wrongs of Woman*, inspired by her mother's adoration of her older brother, 'in comparison with her affection for him, she might be said not to love the rest of her children'.

Of all the children Ned was the only one to receive a 'gentleman's' education, which would prepare him for the Bar. As the family moved around the country from London to Epping, to Yorkshire, back to London, to Wales and finally to London again, the only formal education Mary received was a few years at a day school in Beverley in East Yorkshire where she learned to read and write. From then on everything she learned was self-taught, including several foreign languages.

No wonder such a bright young woman became determined that girls should enjoy the same education as boys. Her hard work and forcefulness did not impress her family, though. She wrote later of her life compared with that of her brother: 'Such indeed is the force of prejudice that what was called spirit and wit in him, was cruelly repressed as forwardness in me.'

There was little opportunity to earn a living for an eighteenth-century middle-class young woman of limited means apart from teaching, becoming a governess, needlework or acting as a lady's companion. Mary tried them all and hated them. Her prospects in the marriage market were poor as there was no money in the family, but then marrying for money would not have fitted her growing political philosophy.

She did attempt to run a girls' school in Newington Green in London in the 1780s. She had rescued her sister Eliza from a brutal marriage and arranged a legal separation for her. They opened the school together in 1784, but it was not a success. Instead she decided to try to become a professional writer.

She was not, as she would describe herself, 'the first of a new genus'. It was not uncommon during this period for women to earn a living by the pen, although the majority were engaged in popular fiction. Mary did not approve, believing the romantic novel to be a dangerous occupation for the young female reading public. Her first work was a stern, moral tract called *Thoughts on the Education of Daughters*, in which she criticised the traditional method of teaching girls, which treated them as inferior to boys. She was delighted to earn £10 from the work and a year later wrote to Eliza, 'I hope you have not forgot that I am an Author.'

It was during her time in Newington Green that she met and befriended a minister, Richard Price. He and a scientist, Joseph Priestley, led a group of intellectuals known as Rational Dissenters. They sought to demystify religion and apply conscience and reason to moral choices. Price became Mary's mentor and, through him, she became acquainted with the leading reformers of the time, including the publisher Joseph Johnson. It was he who commissioned *Thoughts on the Education of Daughters* in 1787. He then published the novel *Mary: A Fiction*, depicting the social limitations oppressing women, and a children's book, *Original Stories from Real Life*. Between 1788 and 1792 she worked for Johnson as a translator and reviewer, helping to found his journal, *Analytical Review*.

Thus she achieved her aim of becoming a pioneer as a liberated woman with the intellectual and financial independence that she advocated for all women. She refused to conform to the demands of high fashion and dressed in a way we would now describe as bohemian. She wore a coarse cloth dress and worsted stockings, wearing her long hair down around her shoulders rather than pinned up as would have been expected of a 'lady'. One disapproving observer described her as 'a philosophical sloven'. She gave up meat and the other 'necessities of life' in order, she said, to better discover the truth of herself. She wrote to one of her women friends, 'Struggle with any obstacles rather than go into a state of dependence . . . I have felt the weight, and would have you by all means avoid it.'

The French Revolution, which began in 1789, became a crucially important event for Mary and her group of liberal intellectuals. She saw it as a struggle for individual liberty against the tyranny of a spoiled and wealthy monarchy and aristocracy. Her friend and mentor, Richard Price, wrote in praise of the revolutionaries and argued that 'the British people, like the French, had the right to remove a bad king from the throne'. He'd earlier been roundly criticised for praising the American Revolution and now the response came from the British states-man Edmund Burke. His heated riposte was called *Reflections on the Revolution in France* and defended the 'inherited rights' of monarchy.

Thomas Paine's response to Burke in 1791, *The Rights of Man*, is probably the better-known work, but Mary was also prompted to respond in support of Price, and of revolution, with a pamphlet entitled 'A Vindication of the Rights of Men', published in 1790. She expressed her opposition to a range of social practices such as the slave trade and addressed human rights and international politics. She also took Burke to task for sympathising with the aristocratic women of France, whom he described as victimised by the Revolution.

'Your tears are reserved,' she wrote, 'very naturally consider-ing your character, for . . . the downfall of queens . . . whilst the distress of many industrious mothers, whose helpmates have been torn from them, and the hungry cry of helpless babes, were vulgar sorrows that could not move your commiseration'.

Her first 'Vindication' was well received by the radicals in London within whom Mary assumed her rightful place, includ-ing William Godwin, Samuel Coleridge, Joseph Priestley, William Blake, Thomas Paine and William Wordsworth. These London radicals were exponents of the Enlightenment – the social revolution that celebrated reason as the absolute core of human identity. They sought to redefine the family, the state and education along the lines of the Enlightenment. It was a short step to the aim of sexual equality for Mary to take as she argued women were the moral and intellectual equals of men in her second Vindication – that of 'the Rights of Woman'.

It took her only three months to produce more than three hundred pages and she was not convinced she had done the best possible job. She wrote to a friend, 'I should have written to you sooner had I not been very much engrossed by writing and printing my vindication of the Rights of Woman . . . I shall give the last sheet to the printer today; and, I am dissatisfied with myself for not having done justice the subject. Do not suspect me of false modesty – I mean to say, that had I allowed myself more time I could have written a better book.'

Nevertheless, the book had an immediate and positive impact. Lady Palmerston is said to have warned her husband, 'I have been reading the rights of Woman, so you must in future expect me to be very tenacious of my rights and privileges.' In Glasgow, a Mrs Anne MacVicar Grant wrote that 'the book was so run after here, that there is no keeping it long enough to read it leisurely'. There were, of course, detractors. The leading evangelical writer and Bluestocking group member Hannah More wrote to Horace Walpole that she had not read the book and found that 'there is something fantastic and absurd in the very title. There is no animal so much indebted to subordination for its good behaviour as woman.' The general opinion of the more conservative women was that the book was an 'Indecent Rhapsody'. One wonders how many of them had actually read it!

Mary was not alone in arguing for women's as well as men's rights. In the midst of the French Revolution, Olympe de Gouges, correctly arguing that Liberté, Égalité and Fraternité rather left out the female perspective, wrote *Declaration of the Rights of Woman and the Female Citizen*, published in 1791, in which she challenged the exclusion of women from the revolutionaries' *Declaration of the Rights of Man*. She was not so well received as Wollstonecraft.

As a result of insisting on women's rights, de Gouges was guillotined on a charge of treason.

Mary's hope that men and women would successfully achieve equality in their education and, consequently, their relationships with each other did not quite work out for her. She had pleaded in *A Vindication* for intellectual companionship to be the ideal of marriage, with women able to be defined by their own character and work rather than by their marriages. When it came to men, she failed to practise what she preached. In London she had fallen passionately in love with a painter and literary figure called Henry Fuseli. He was married and his wife was unaware of their affair. Mary, never one for concealing her feelings, and often more likely to jump into a situation with both feet rather than consider the consequences, decided they should be open about the relationship. She went round to Fuseli's home, asked to see his wife, Sophia, and informed her that the best solution to their dilemma was a ménage à trois. Sophia was furious, thought Mary's plan appalling and threw her out of the house. The affair was over.

In 1792, as her feminist manifesto hit the bookshops, Mary travelled to France, ostensibly to witness the Revolution that had so inspired her, but, rather conveniently, escaping London and the Fuseli scandal. She arrived just as the Jacobin Terror, which would see mass executions and the rise of arbitrary power, was about to begin. Her book, *An Historical and Moral View of the Origin and Progress of the French Revolution*, published in 1794, documents her attempts to reconcile her horror at the violence with her belief in the perfectibility of man. Her disillusionment was profound.

In France, in the midst of political chaos and, as an Englishwoman, great physical danger, Mary lost her heart again. In Paris she was welcomed into a group of British and American free-thinking radicals and, in the early months of 1793, she met Captain Gilbert Imlay. He was handsome, charming, a former soldier now involved in trade, and Mary fell hopelessly in love.

In November of the same year she wrote to him: 'I have felt some gentle twitches, which make me begin to think, that I am nourishing a creature who will soon be sensible of my care. This thought has . . . produced an overflowing of tenderness to you.'

Imlay did not share her overflowing of tenderness, but he did protect her from the possibility of imprisonment as an Englishwoman as the unrest continued by registering her as his wife at the American Embassy. (They had not actually married.) Americans were protected from the Terror by their nationality, but he soon went off on commercial travels, leaving Mary alone. She followed him to Le Havre, hoping that the birth of their child would bring him closer to her. Fanny was born there in May 1794. Imlay would not become the devoted father she had hoped for.

She named her daughter Fanny after her closest friend from childhood, Fanny Blood. William Godwin, in his book about Mary written after her death, said that she and Fanny 'contracted a friendship so fervent as for years to have constituted the ruling passion of her mind'. There is no evidence to suggest that theirs was a sexual relationship, but the two women lived and worked together for ten years and Mary virtually adopted Fanny's family as her own.

In 1785 Fanny had travelled to Lisbon to marry an Irishman who lived there. She became pregnant and Mary went to Lisbon to be with her at the time of the birth. Fanny died in childbirth and Godwin wrote that Mary had named her daughter Fanny after 'the dear friend of her youth, whose image could never be erased from her memory'.

After her daughter's birth, Mary followed Imlay to London where she hoped they would set up a family home together. He was busy with his commercial ventures, beginning to see other women and had no interest in family life. Mary made her first attempt at suicide by taking an overdose of opium, but was found and revived by a maid.

The miserable relationship dragged on. It seems astonishing that such a rational, clever woman could have allowed herself to be used and abused by such a man, but, when he asked her to go to Norway to sort out a business problem for him she packed her bag and, with her tiny baby and a maid, set out for Scandinavia. She spent several months negotiating for compensation for a cargo of Imlay's that had been stolen by the Norwegian captain of his ship.

When she returned to London she was told by her cook that Imlay had another new mistress – an actress – and Mary made her second attempt at suicide. She walked to Putney Bridge and threw herself into the River Thames, but was rescued by two passing boatmen. Still she tried to revive the relationship with Imlay, constantly pleading for reconciliation. She gave up hope in 1796 when she wrote her last letter to him. 'I now solemnly assure you this is an eternal farewell . . . I part with you in peace.'

When Mary had first met William Godwin, the author of *An Enquiry Concerning Political Justice*, and one of the leading radicals of the time, it had been at a dinner party at Joseph Johnson's house in 1791. The two had argued about religion and appeared to dislike each other. But then, in 1796, soon after she ended her relationship with Imlay, Mary made the first move on Godwin – not the sort of thing expected of a late-eighteenth-century woman! She went to his house, ostensibly to lend him a book, and they quickly began a highly charged erotic relationship.

Mary's letters to Godwin bubble with obvious delight at their physical passion for each other. In November 1796 she wrote to him, 'If the felicity of last night has had the same effect on your health as on my countenance, you have no cause to lament your failure of resolution for I have seldom seen so much live fire running about my features as this morning when recollections – very dear; called forth the blush of pleasure, as I adjusted my hair.'

Wollstonecraft and Godwin did not intend to marry – both had political reservations about the marital state and it was generally assumed, as Mary continued to use the name Imlay, that she had been married in Paris. But early in 1797 Mary discovered she was pregnant and the two decided to wed, causing yet another scandal as so many of their friends had assumed she was already married. A number dropped her, shocked that Fanny had been born out of wedlock.

Mary and Godwin seem to have achieved the kind of marriage she had hoped for. She moved into his house in Somers Town in London and he rented a study for use during the day. They wrote and visited friends, often separately, as both were keen to retain their independence, and Mary looked forward to the arrival of the child she called, in advance of 'his' arrival, 'little William'.

She gave birth on 30 August to Mary – later Shelley and the author of *Frankenstein* – but the placenta had to be removed manually by the midwife, causing the puerperal fever from which she died eleven days after her labour.

Godwin wrote to a friend that he believed he would never find happiness again, but he did manage to write a memoir of his wife only two years after her death in which he detailed her sexual exploits. It did nothing to enhance her reputation, but no doubt made him and the two girls a pretty penny. Life, as they say, is copy.

The memoir led to some condemnation of Wollstonecraft, notably by the nineteenth-century sociologist Harriet Martineau, who wrote:

Women who would improve the condition and chances of their sex must, I am certain, be not only affectionate and devoted, but rational and dispassionate ... But Mary Wollstonecraft was, with all her powers, a poor victim of passion, with no control over her own peace, and no calmness or content except when the needs of her individual nature were satisfied.

Later in the nineteenth century, as we have seen, she was championed as an exponent of total equality between the sexes by suffragists and educationalists such as Millicent Garrett Fawcett and Barbara Bodichon and, by the twentieth century, as attitudes to sex became more liberal, she had become the feminist hero she is today. Virginia Woolf summed up her impact:

> She whose sense of her own existence was so intense, who had cried out even in her misery, 'I cannot bear to think of being no more – of losing myself – nay, it appears to be impossible that I should cease to exist,' died at the age of thirty-six [*sic*; she was thirty-eight]. But she has her revenge. Many millions have died and been forgotten in the hundred and thirty years that have passed since she was buried; and yet as we read her letters and listen to her arguments and consider her experiments, above all, that most fruitful experiment, her relation with Godwin, and realise the high-handed and hot-blooded manner in which she cut her way to the quick of life, one form of immortality is hers undoubtedly; she is alive and active, she argues and experiments, we hear her voice and trace her influence even now among the living.

'Let other pens dwell on guilt and misery.'

*Mansfield Park*

# 7

# Jane Austen

## 1775–1817

This was a really difficult choice to make. Of all the great novelists who've delighted me over the years, which would best fit into the title *A History of Britain in 21 Women*? Should it be Charlotte Brontë, whose *Jane Eyre* is such an important story for girls who are powerless and suffer deprivation and abuse?

I could have chosen George Eliot. She was born Mary Ann Evans, but took a man's name for her writing to avoid being stereotyped as a female creator of romances, typical of her period, and lived, unmarried, with George Henry Lewes; not the way to behave in nineteenth-century Britain. Her masterpiece *Middlemarch* provides a portrait of life in mid-nineteenth-century provincial England. It's set against a backdrop of widespread social unrest and economic change. Her central character, Dorothea Brooke, is a clever, beautiful idealist who helps the poor and marries the wrong man, but finds happiness after his death in a marriage founded on an equal partnership.

A third choice might have been Mrs Gaskell. I would prefer to name her, as she deserved, by her own name rather than as a mere adjunct to her husband. She was Elizabeth Gaskell. Her novels *Mary Barton* and *North and South* were, perhaps, the most obviously political books of any woman writing in English as she uncovered the harsh conditions of the working class in the mills of Manchester.

I have, though, opted for Jane Austen because for me she typifies everything I love about being British. She is overtly critical of anything of which she disapproves, from snobbishness to cruelty to social climbing. She is supremely observant and witty and uses the English language in the most elegant way possible. Who else could have begun a novel (*Pride and Prejudice*) with the words, 'It is a truth universally acknowledged that a single man in possession of a good fortune, must be in want of a wife', leaving unsaid the obvious corollary that a single woman with no fortune must be in want of a rich husband to raise her status in life?

It was not an aim she followed, preferring to try to make her living and support her family through her writing. Indeed, the one opportunity she had to marry and improve her family's finances she turned down. In 1802 she received the only proposal of marriage we know about. She met Harris Bigg-Wither through some old friends, Alethea, Elizabeth and Catherine Bigg. He was their younger brother and they met during a visit by Jane and her sister, Cassandra, to the Biggs' home in Basingstoke. Harris had completed his education at Oxford and had enjoyed good prospects. He was also the heir to considerable family estates, though he was not, according to descriptions by Jane's niece, Caroline, an attractive man: 'very plain in person – awkward and even uncouth in manner . . . nothing but his size to recommend him . . . one need not look about for secret reasons to account for a young lady's not loving him'.

At first Jane accepted his proposal, but, having slept on her decision, withdrew. There are no letters from the time explaining why she decided she wouldn't marry him. It must have been a difficult decision, because the marriage would have given her a substantial income and enabled her to provide her parents and her sister with a comfortable home.

Sadly, the majority of her letters have been lost. It's estimated that only 160 of some three thousand letters she wrote still exist. Her sister burned the majority of those she had received from Jane and is thought to have censored the rest. Others were destroyed by her brother, Francis. Most of what is known about her life comes from biographies written by relatives some fifty years after her death when her popularity as a novelist began to increase. We must accept that there may be a degree of bias in what they wrote, portraying her primarily as 'good quiet Aunt Jane'.

There is, though, a letter which she sent to her niece, Fanny Knight, in 1814. Fanny had asked her aunt for advice about a relationship. Jane responded, 'having written so much on one side of the question, I shall now turn round and entreat you not to commit yourself farther, and not to think of accepting him unless you really do like him. Anything is to be preferred or endured rather than marrying without Affection.'

Jane Austen was born to George Austen, an Anglican rector, and his wife, Cassandra. They were not themselves well off, although they both came from substantial families. The Austens had been wool manufacturers and landowners, while Cassandra was a member of the aristocratic Leigh family. For much of Jane's life her father was the priest at Steventon in Hampshire, adding to his income from the Church by teaching boys who boarded at the Austen vicarage.

There were eight children in the Austen family: James, George, Edward, Henry Thomas, Cassandra, Frank, Charles John and Jane. Cassandra, named after her mother, would be Jane's closest friend and confidante throughout her life.

As a baby, Jane was farmed out, presumably to a wet nurse, in the village. Elizabeth Littlewood nursed her and cared for her for some eighteen months. At the age of eight, she was sent away to Oxford with her sister – now ten – to be educated by a Mrs Ann Cawley, the sister of one of her uncles. They moved with Mrs

Cawley to Southampton later in 1783 and it was there that both girls caught typhus. Jane nearly died and it's possible that her relatively early death, at the age of only forty-one, may have been connected to such a serious childhood illness.

The girls returned home to Steventon and, for a couple of years, continued their education there. There's a reference in *Northanger Abbey* to Catherine Morland enjoying 'rolling down the green slope at the back of the house' and preferring cricket to girls' play. Maybe, with so many brothers, it's the kind of game Jane and her sister may have enjoyed.

In 1785 the Austen girls were sent as boarders to Abbey House School in Reading, which is again said to have had a place in Jane's writing. It's believed to have resembled Mrs Goddard's casual school, which appears in *Emma*. Jane, at ten, was thought to be a little young to benefit from the level of education on offer at the Abbey, but her mother was reluctant to separate the sisters. She is quoted as saying, 'If Cassandra were going to have her head cut off, Jane would insist on sharing her fate.'

They spent just a year at the school as their parents could no longer afford to pay the fees. It was the only real education Jane had outside the family. They returned home to Steventon and learned the piano and drawing – as was expected of an accomplished young lady of the period – but Jane also had access to her father's extensive library. She wrote that she and her family were 'great novel readers and not ashamed of being so'.

She was familiar with the works of Henry Fielding and Samuel Richardson and was a great fan of Fanny Burney. The title for *Pride and Prejudice* came from a phrase in Burney's novel *Cecilia*, and when Burney's *Camilla*, came out in 1796 one of the subscribers was 'Miss J Austen, Steventon'. In *Northanger Abbey* she made a 'defence of the novel' and the three books she included were Burney's *Cecilia* and *Camilla*, and Maria Edgeworth's *Belinda*.

Between 1787 and 1793 Jane wrote what she later called her Juvenilia, including lots of humorous parodies of the popular novels of the day. They were generally dedicated to members of the family and written only for their amusement. It's clear that the atmosphere in the Austen household was one of loving relationships and an insistence on the importance of a good education for both girls and boys, even if lack of money meant the education had to take place at home. Plays were performed, books were read and discussed, and no one in the family seems to have been afraid to give an opinion and argue with anyone who may have disagreed. It's clear that Jane's ideas and her wit were fostered at home.

It was during these early years, from 1795 to 1799, that the first versions of the novels that would eventually be published as *Sense and Sensibility*, *Pride and Prejudice* and *Northanger Abbey* were created. *Pride and Prejudice*, now probably her best-known and most popular novel, was originally called 'First Impressions' and was rejected by the publisher to whom her father offered it. He had not, apparently, even looked at it. Bet he kicked himself when he realised his mistake.

When we read of dances and parties in the novels, it's obvious that Jane had plenty of experience of the kind of social life that was on offer in Hampshire. There's an odd description of Jane by an observer, Mrs Mitford, that casts her as 'the prettiest, silliest, most affected, husband-hunting butterfly' Mrs Mitford ever remembered. There is, though, hardly any evidence of any flirtatious courtships with men. There is one letter to Cassandra, written over a couple of days, which does make reference to Thomas Lefroy, an impecunious Irish relative of one of Jane's old friends, Anne Lefroy, and there was a mutual flirtation between them.

Jane was twenty when she wrote:

Tell Mary that I make over Mr. Heartley and all his Estate to her for her sole use and Benefit in future, and not only him, but all my other Admirers into the bargain wherever she can find them, even the kiss which C. Powlett wanted to give me, as I mean to confine myself in future to Mr. Tom Lefroy, for whom I don't care sixpence . . .

Friday – At length the Day is come on which I am to flirt my last with Tom Lefroy, and when you receive this it will be over. My tears flow as I write at the melancholy idea.

It was known that Tom Lefroy could not afford to marry Jane. Years later, when he became Chief Justice of Ireland, he confessed to his nephew that he had 'a boyish love for Jane Austen'.

Jane had known Bath and Southampton from occasional visits, but it was in late 1800, when her father was seventy, that he decided to retire and move the family to Bath, the spa town and favourite recreational haunt of Georgian Britain. It was not Jane's choice of home.

During their years in the city, lasting until her father's death in 1805, the family spent the summer at the seaside and it was in South Devonshire, west of Lyme Regis, that Jane seems to have had a holiday romance. We don't know the name of the young man, but many years later Cassandra would tell her nieces of someone she had considered a suitable suitor who had fallen in love with Jane. She said, 'They parted – but he made it plain he should seek them out again.'

Soon after, they heard of his death and there's been much speculation that elements of this incident may have appeared in *Persuasion*. Jane, at the time of the encounter, would have been twenty-seven, the same age as *Persuasion*'s Anne Elliot, and significant scenes take place in Lyme Regis. The novel was written towards the end of her life and it has a sadder and, at times, more bitterly ironic tone than her earlier works. Austen's biographer Claire Tomalin characterises the book as Austen's 'present to herself, to Miss Sharp, to Cassandra, to Martha Lloyd . . . to all women who had lost their chance in life and would never enjoy a second spring'. Miss Sharp was the friend to whom Jane sent signed first editions of her novels. Martha Lloyd was Jane's closest friend after Cassandra, but Jane's prediction of her having no second spring was mistaken. In 1823, six years after Jane's death, her brother Frank's wife died in childbirth and in 1828 he married Martha. By now Frank, the naval officer, had been knighted. Martha was sixty-two when she became Lady Austen.

Anne Elliot, of course, also has a second spring. She had been persuaded to break off her engagement to the impecunious Captain Wentworth in her youth when her family was well off. As her family's fortunes diminish she meets him again. Wentworth overhears Anne saying women never give up their feelings of love, even when all hope is lost and they are happily reconciled.

In 1805 the Reverend Austen died and what little income the remaining family – Mrs Austen and the two daughters – had was significantly reduced as his clerical living lapsed with his death. The family was now dependent on handouts from the brothers and a small legacy left to Cassandra by her former fiancé. Her love life, like Jane's, had no happy ending. Thomas Fowle had been one of Reverend Austen's pupils, who went on to graduate from Oxford University. In 1794 he proposed to Cassandra, was accepted, but needed to earn some money before he could afford to get married. He took a job as chaplain to a military expedition to the Caribbean, but died there from yellow fever in 1797, leaving Cassandra £1,000 in his will.

Mrs Austen, Jane, Cassandra and Martha Lloyd set up home together, first in Southampton, close to two of the brothers who would become Admirals in the Navy, and later, in 1809, in Chawton in Hampshire. The house was provided by her brother Edward on one of his estates. Jane was delighted to have left Bath with 'what happy feelings of escape', as she put it in a letter to Cassandra, and pleased to be back in Hampshire, not far from their old home in Steventon.

In Chawton she resumed her literary career and began by

revising *Sense and Sensibility*. It was accepted by a publisher in late 1810, but 'at her own risk'. It appeared anonymously, 'By a Lady', and at first only her immediate family knew the name of the author. Jane's niece, Fanny Knight, records in her diary for September 1811 a 'letter from Aunt Cass to beg we would not mention that Aunt Jane wrote *Sense and Sensibility*'. There was also an incident in a 'circulating' library in Alton in 1812, which Jane, Cassandra and their niece, Anna, were visiting. Anna's mother threw down a copy of *Sense and Sensibility* on offer there, 'exclaiming to the great amusement of the Aunts who stood by "Oh, that must be rubbish I am sure from the title."'

There were a couple of favourable reviews of the novel and Jane made a profit of £140. She was encouraged to continue with her writing and next began revising 'First Impressions', which would become *Pride and Prejudice*, the now incredibly famous story of Elizabeth Bennet and the rocky road to love for her and Mr Darcy. When *Woman's Hour* carried out a survey of which book listeners would count as the one that had most influence on them, *Pride and Prejudice* won hands down. Jane called it her 'own darling child' and it was published in 1813. It was around this time that the name of the author became known. As she wrote in a letter soon after publication, 'Henry heard P and P warmly praised in Scotland by Lady Robert Kerr and another lady; and what does he do in the warmth of his Brotherly vanity and Love, but immediately tell them who wrote it!'

She had sold the copyright for *Pride and Prejudice* for £110, so didn't receive anything extra when a second edition was published soon after the first. As a second edition of *Sense and Sensibility* was printed and *Mansfield Park* appeared in May 1814, she had sensibly engaged the services of her brother Henry as a kind of agent, and she sometimes stayed in his house in London to revise her proof sheets.

Jane's secrecy in relation to her work is legendary. In

Steventon she had had a private dressing room in which she could write her Juvenilia and the early versions of the first three novels undisturbed. In Chawton she had no such private writing space and another of her brothers, James Edward, told the story of the 'creaking door'. She asked for it not to be fixed as it gave her warning of any approaching visitors and she could hide whatever manuscript she was working on before they came into the room.

Jane continued her literary work at Chawton, although she would never achieve the recognition she deserved during her life-time. *Emma* appeared in 1815, dedicated to the Prince Regent, who was, evidently, a fan. A second edition of *Mansfield Park* did not do well and her losses on the reprint ate up most of her profits on *Emma*. *Northanger Abbey* and *Persuasion* were published posthumously.

During these final years of her life Jane often visited her brothers and their children, taking her role as aunt very seriously. When one of her nieces, Caroline Craven Austen, became an aunt, Jane wrote to her, 'Now that you are become an Aunt, you are a person of some consequence and must excite great Interest whatever you do. I have always maintained the importance of Aunts as much as possible, and I am sure of your doing the same now.'

She was, though, very conscious of her age and her spinster status. In a letter of 1813, when she was thirty-seven, she wrote, 'By the bye, as I must leave off being young, I find many Douceurs in being a sort of Chaperon for I am put on the Sofa near the Fire and can drink as much wine as I like.' A few days earlier she had written, 'I bought a concert ticket and a sprig of flowers for my old age.' I suspect she was often depressed and I'm convinced that this state of mind had a great influence on *Emma*, always my favourite Jane Austen novel, which I read for the first time at school, as it was on the syllabus for O-level English Literature.

Jane described the character she was about to create thusly: 'I am going to take a heroine whom no one but myself will much like.' In the first sentence she introduces 'Emma Woodhouse, handsome, clever and rich' and, like Jane, I adored her. I delighted in the way she messed up her matchmaking with her complete lack of sensitivity to anyone else's feelings, always letting her imagination run riot. But she has wonderful qualities. She cares deeply for her father, she only wants everyone to be happy and she learns her lesson.

In the most telling scene in the book, when everyone goes on the picnic to Box Hill, Emma is joshing with Frank Churchill and insults Miss Bates – the friendly, rather garrulous spinster with whom, I suspect, Jane Austen greatly sympathises. Emma, the only Austen heroine who has no money worries, is roundly ticked off about her appalling manners by her neighbour, Mr Knightley. She's ashamed, makes amends, and she and Mr Knightley are married with the prospect of 'perfect happiness'. As is always the case for Jane a successful marriage must come with mutual respect, admiration and companionship, not simply romantic passion.

It was, tragically for her and for her sister, something neither of them achieved. Early in 1816 Jane began to feel unwell. She continued to work – *Sanditon*, her last attempt at a novel, was not finished, but was eventually published in 1925. Her health deteriorated rapidly over the coming year and in 1817, only forty-one years old, she died. Lots of theories about the reason for her early demise have been put forward over the years, the most bizarre of which came from the crime writer Lyndsay Ashford, who found a letter in which Jane described 'recovering my Looks a little, which have been bad enough, black and white and every wrong colour'. These are, apparently, classic signs of arsenic poisoning. One of Jane's biographers, Professor Janet Todd, dismisses the idea that Jane may have been murdered, but accepts that arsenic may have been involved. It was often present in medication in the eighteenth and nineteenth centuries and Jane may well have taken such a medicine for her rheumatism.

Jane had refused to take her illness seriously, but as she became unable to walk she was taken by Henry and Cassandra to Winchester for treatment. It was there that she died and Henry, thanks to his clerical connections, was able to arrange her burial in the north aisle of the nave in Winchester Cathedral. The inscription on her tombstone makes no mention of her novels, but a brass tablet, added later, refers to her as 'known to many by her writings'.

I worked in Southampton in the early part of my journalistic career and often went to Winchester to visit her. I wish I could have made her hear how much her work had meant to me and to millions of others, whether they read her or saw her works on film or television. There may only be six complete novels, but they are truly great.

'Age has not abated my zeal for the emancipation of my sex from the unreasonable prejudice too prevalent in Great Britain against a literary and scientific education for women.'

Mary Somerville

# 8

# Mary Somerville

## 1780–1872

In February 2016 the Royal Bank of Scotland organised a vote to decide which of three notable Scots should appear on its new £10 bank note. In most countries it's only governments, through their central banks, that are permitted to issue currency, but in Scotland three clearing banks – Bank of Scotland, Clydesdale Bank and RBS – are still allowed to issue bank notes.

The three possible candidates were the physicist James Clerk Maxwell, the civil engineer Thomas Telford and the scientist, science writer and translator Mary Somerville. Somerville won by a significant majority.

Mary Fairfax, as she was called before her marriage, was born in 1780 in her aunt's house in Jedburgh in the Scottish Borders. She grew up in the family home in Burntisland on the Firth of Forth, not far from Edinburgh. She had few expectations apart from a genteel life within her small family circle with little education apart from the usual female accomplishments of sewing, music and painting.

Mary's mother, Margaret Charters, was from a well-to-do Scottish family, but had no money of her own. Her father, William George Fairfax, was a naval officer who rose to the rank of Admiral and was knighted, but he was not a wealthy man. He earned a modest salary from service in the American War of

Independence and in British service overseas, a career in which he saw Britain lose its first empire in America and build another in the East Indies. Her elder brother, Sam, also contributed to British Imperialism. He began a promising career in India, but died of fever there at the age of only twenty-one. There was no money in the family for a tutor or governess for Mary.

Her circumstances have been described as 'genteel poverty'. She was allowed to run pretty wild in the coastal countryside around her home and, like her father, she became fascinated with natural history. He was passionate about plants and particularly tulips, while she studied the sea shells, birds and flowers that she found around her. She was also expected to fulfil the role of a growing daughter in a well-connected family. She attended lots of social events, was sweet and polite, and dubbed 'the Rose of Jedburgh' by their social circle.

By the age of eight she had not yet been taught to write and the next few years of her education did not advance her very far. When she was ten and her father, Sir William, came home from sea, he described his daughter as 'a savage' and sent her for a year of tuition at an expensive boarding school in Musselburgh. She returned home able to read and write, but not very well, to perform simple arithmetic and speak a little French. But she did find a magazine in the house that consisted mainly of fashion plates, and in it there was an article about algebra. From that point on she was passionate about mathematics and spent her time looking for books that would further her knowledge and understanding.

She was taught informally at home and her lessons included elementary geography and astronomy, while her uncle, who described her as an eager student, was engaged to teach her Latin. Mary was furious to find her education was extremely limited compared with what her brother was receiving. On one occasion she was listening in when he was being tutored in mathematics and was able to answer when he couldn't. The tutor was impressed and agreed to teach her unofficially.

After the death of her younger sister at the age of ten, Mary was banned by her parents from receiving any further education. They believed that too much intellectual activity had contributed to her sister's death. Naturally no such constraints applied to the boys and Mary continued to teach herself in secret.

Her other talent, apart from maths, was for painting. She had lessons at a school in Edinburgh and there learned about perspective, which she found inspiring, but in a mathematical sense – she sought out a copy of Euclid's *Elements of Geometry* and taught herself from it. She enjoyed her art and she clearly impressed one of her mother's rather grand relatives with her paintings. The aunt observed that it was fortunate that Mary had such a talent because she would be able to earn her living by her painting, 'for everyone knows she will not have a sixpence'.

Much later in her life Mary wrote of these comments:

Had it been my lot to win my bread by painting, I fear I should have fared badly, but I never should have been ashamed of it; on the contrary, I should have been very proud had I been successful. I must say the idea of making money had never entered my head . . . but I was intensely ambitious to excel in something, for I felt in my own breast that women were capable of taking a higher place in creation than that assigned to them in my early days, which was very low.

Mary was born into the age of the Scottish Enlightenment. As a young debutante staying in Edinburgh she sought out the friends of her brother and father, begging them for more lessons in Latin, algebra, geology and natural history. She was now moving among Edinburgh's intelligentsia – the heirs of Adam Smith and David Hume, and the founders of the intellectual journal of the day, the *Edinburgh Review*.

There was a minor setback when, in 1804, at the age of twenty-four, she married a distant cousin, Samuel Greig, who held the post of Russian Consul in London. He did not approve of her intellectual pursuits and she quickly had two sons. It was, perhaps, fortunate for her and for science that Greig died only three years after they were married. She returned to her family in Burntisland, an impoverished widow with two infants, one of whom she was still nursing.

At home, before she had to begin her duties as a mother and daughter, she rose early in the morning to study trigonometry and astronomy and grappled with understanding Newton's *Principia*. In Edinburgh she made contact with the leading mathematicians William and John Wallace and persuaded them to recommend to her the scientific books, all in French, that she needed to continue her studies. She befriended Henry Brougham, then a rising politician who later became Lord Chancellor and founder of the University of London, and she began to make original scientific observations of her own.

In 1812 she married again, this time to an older cousin, Dr William Somerville. He was a naval physician and theirs was a very happy marriage. He paid no attention to the friends and family members who disapproved loudly of Mary's work and characterised her openly as eccentric and foolish. He encouraged her scientific research, which she managed to fit around the birth of four more children, and often expressed his pride in her achievements. He himself became a Fellow of the Royal Society, a status his wife could only enjoy in an honorary capacity as women were not admitted. Early in her career, her paper 'On the Magnetizing Power of the More Refrangible Solar Rays' had to be read to the Royal Society by William, as women were not allowed to attend its meetings.

The Somervilles lived in relative comfort in London, with servants, but they had their share of tragedy. Both their sons died in infancy and their eldest daughter, Margaret, passed away at the age of nine. They also had periods of serious illness themselves, but they enjoyed a sparkling social life among the leading writers, thinkers and liberal politicians of their time.

The Irish novelist Maria Edgeworth said of her in 1822, 'Laplace says she is the only woman in England who understands his works.' Pierre-Simon Laplace was an influential French mathematician who was important in the development of statistics, physics and astronomy. Lady Byron, who had walked away from her marriage to the libertine poet Lord Byron soon after their daughter was born, asked Mary to tutor the girl who became Ada Lovelace, renowned as one of the founders of computer science and the subject of another chapter in this book. The painter J. M. W. Turner was a good friend and admirer of Somerville. She was a frequent visitor to his studio, and wrote about the sunsets over Lake Albino in Italy: 'The sunsets were glorious and I, fascinated by the gorgeous colouring, attempted to paint what Turner alone could have done justice.'

The time in which Somerville lived has been described as the 'Age of Wonder'. Britain had emerged from the Napoleonic Wars as the undisputed great power of the nineteenth century. It was the first industrial nation, and while London simmered with social unrest, deprivation, dirt and sickness, the intellectual life of the capital was fizzing.

There was experiment in every field – politics, the arts, science and engineering. Sir Robert Peel, as Home Secretary, introduced what would become the Metropolitan Police. Lord Liverpool's Conservative government got rid of capital punishment for all crimes apart from treason, murder and arson. The workhouse, mass schools for the poor, gas lighting, the railways and a metropolitan sewage system all happened during Mary's lifetime and all, to a Victorian, denoted tremendous progress. In her memoirs she said how extraordinary was the speed of travel and communication in the 'steam age'.

In 1827 Mary's friend Henry Brougham was in the process of

founding his 'Society for Diffusing Useful Knowledge'. He wrote to William asking him to persuade his wife to translate from French Laplace's seminal work of astronomy, *Mécanique Céleste*. 'No one without trying it,' he wrote, 'can conceive how far we may carry ignorant readers into an understanding of the depths of science.' Only Mary Somerville, he thought, could do it.

In her memoirs Mary wrote how much the letter had surprised her:

> I thought Lord Brougham must have been mistaken with regard to my acquirements, and naturally concluded that my self-acquired knowledge was so far inferior to that of the men who had been educated in our universities that it would be the height of presumption to attempt to write on such a subject, or indeed on any other.

Brougham refused to take no for an answer and travelled to Chelsea to persuade her in person. She agreed to carry out the task on condition that, if the work were not good enough, it should be burned. It *was* good enough and, as she put it in her memoirs, 'Thus suddenly and unexpectedly the whole character and course of my future life was changed.'

Among the Somervilles' best friends were the renowned astronomer Sir John Herschel (nephew of Caroline) and his wife. After he had read *The Mechanism of the Heavens*, which would become a huge bestseller, Mary received a letter from Herschel expressing his highest admiration for her achievement. 'Go on thus,' he wrote, 'and you will leave a memorial of no common kind to posterity.'

More than a mere translation, the book was a highly significant exposition of the state of modern science. It was too long for Brougham's series of popular educational tracts for which it had been intended and instead was published in 1831 by John Murray and was an instant success.

Three years later Mary Somerville published her second

major scientific work, *On the Connexion of the Physical Sciences*. It was the publisher's most successful book on science until Murray published Darwin's *On the Origin of Species* some twenty-five years later.

She was in her fifties when she published the two books, and she had managed to make a clear explanation of scientific discoveries up to that date, making the links between them comprehensible for a general audience. She spent months in conversation with leading scientists in Britain and France, ranging from astronomers and physicists to geologists, geographers and chemists, and explored subjects ranging from terrestrial magnetism to giant seaweed. One chapter was based on her own research into infrared and ultraviolet rays, one of the earliest descriptions of these phenomena. This research was demonstrated in the recent Mike Leigh film, *Mr Turner*, in a scene where Mary Somerville tries to show the artist how the rays from the sun could create a magnetic field – a classic moment of science meeting art!

Somerville possessed the great quality of being open to new scientific possibilities and was able to convey her curiosity in her writing. She fascinated readers who were not necessarily scientists by reporting on the extraordinary new discoveries of the time and opening their minds to potential future developments. She speculated about planets that had not yet been observed, the mechanism by which climate might change and the causes of earthquakes, opening up lots of questions for future research. Richard Holmes, the author of *The Age of Wonder: How the Romantic Generation Discovered the Beauty and Terror of Science*, says that it was Somerville's work that 'prompted the creation of a new professional concept, and new umbrella term to define it, coined by Whewell in his review of 1834: "scientist"'. She was, then, the first person to be called a scientist.

Her third book, *Physical Geography*, was published in 1848 and was the first English-language textbook in this area, introducing an innovative regional approach to geography. It featured on university reading lists, including Oxford's, for decades and led eventually to the award of the Victoria Gold Medal of the Royal Geographical Society, one of the many awards and accolades Mary received, which had begun with the honorary membership of the Royal Society. The government rewarded her with an annual pension of £200, increased later to £300, which came in very handy when her husband lost all his money in a poor investment. The couple and their two unmarried daughters, Martha and Mary Charlotte, spent most of their later years in Italy, travelling all over Europe to meet scientists and writers to discuss their most recent works.

Throughout her life Mary had been an example of what a woman could achieve from her own efforts, but how galling it must have been to be awarded only honorary membership of the Royal Society and to be forced to publish her first work in her husband's name. She had been a wife, mother and leading scientist, honoured throughout Europe at a time when it was common to argue, as her own parents had done, that education made women morally and physically unfit for motherhood.

But the campaign for women's suffrage was growing in the middle of the century and Mary gave her active support to the movement. She was asked to be the lead signatory on John Stuart Mill's petition for votes for women, which was presented to Parliament more than fifty years before limited suffrage was won in the Representation of the People Act of 1918.

In her final years she wrote in her memoirs, 'Age has not abated my zeal for the emancipation of my sex from the unreasonable prejudice too prevalent in Great Britain against a literary and scientific education for women.' She drove home the point by praising the French and the Russians for granting degrees to women.

Despite her great age her intellect was as keen as ever, for which she expressed her thanks, and she continued to be interested in scientific progress.

Though far advanced in years, I take as lively an interest as ever in passing events. I regret I shall not live to know the results of the expedition to determine the currents of the ocean, the distance of the earth from the sun determined by the transits of Venus, and the source of the most renowned of rivers, the discovery of which will immortalise the name of Dr. Livingstone.

Somerville passed her extreme old age studying calculus and keeping up with events through the newspapers. She spent 29 November 1872 working on the complex mathematical system known as quaternions and died in her sleep that night, less than a month before her ninety-second birthday. Only seven years after her death Oxford University opened its second women's college, calling it Somerville. If only she could have been there to see it.

'I am a Creole, and have good Scotch blood
coursing through my veins. My father was
a soldier, of an old Scottish family . . . I
have a few shades of deeper brown upon
my skin which shows me related – and I am
proud of the relationship – to those poor
mortals whom you once held enslaved,
and whose bodies America still owns.'

Mary Seacole

# 9

# Mary Seacole

## 1805–1881

It's generally assumed that the profession of nursing owes its respectability to Florence Nightingale, usually known as the true heroine of the Crimean War, but her place has recently been somewhat superseded by Mary Seacole, voted in 2004 to head the list of 100 Great Black Britons.

In 2012 St Thomas' Hospital in London announced plans to erect a massive statue of the Jamaican-born Mary Seacole across the river from the Houses of Parliament, and to call her the 'Pioneer Nurse'. This despite Nightingale's long association with the hospital, which was her base for more than forty years and from where the Nightingale Faculty of Nursing and Midwifery operates.

Since the announcement of the statue there's been bitter rivalry between the Nightingale and Seacole camps, and there can be no doubt that, of the two, it was Nightingale who documented the work she had done at the Scutari hospital in the Crimea, and the terrible death toll, from which a great deal was learned about the correct way to treat soldiers during conflict. It was also she who, with an established position in British society, was able to achieve training for nurses and great influence over the way hospital nursing should be run.

I refuse to enter into the competition as both these women are worthy of their place in Britain's history. I do, though, aim to commemorate a woman who had none of Nightingale's wealth or social advantages, but still managed to take herself to a war zone and use whatever knowledge and skill she had to care for the wounded soldiers there, at the same time as facing clear racial prejudice.

If Nightingale was the Lady with the Lamp, Seacole's nom de guerre was 'Mother Seacole'. She was born Mary Grant in Kingston, Jamaica. Her father was a Scottish soldier and her mother a free Jamaican woman who was known as a 'doctress'. She was a healer who used Caribbean and African traditional remedies at the same time as running a hotel. In Mary's auto-biography, *The Wonderful Adventures of Mrs Seacole In Many Lands* (the title suggests she may have been prone to self-promotion and some exaggeration), she says that she learned her nursing at her mother's side, first practising on her doll, then her pets, and then helping her mother with patients.

As far as her race is concerned, she described herself as Creole: 'I am a Creole, and have good Scotch blood coursing through my veins. My father was a soldier, of an old Scottish family . . . I have a few shades of deeper brown upon my skin which shows me related – and I am proud of the relationship – to those poor mortals whom you once held enslaved, and whose bodies America still owns.' Slavery was not fully abolished in Jamaica until 1838. She was careful in her autobiography to describe what a vigorous and hard-working woman she was, clearly at pains to point out that she does not fit the stereotype of the 'lazy Creole'.

It's likely that Mary held quite a high position in Jamaican society as her father was respected as a member of the British Army and her mother was a well-known businesswoman. She also spent some time during her childhood in the home of what she described as her 'kind patroness'. She was treated as a member of the family in this elderly person's house and, as a result, received a good education.

In her late teens Mary went to London to visit relatives. Although there were a number of black people living in the city at that time, Mary made a note of the kind of racial abuse that could happen. A West Indian man of her acquaintance who, she said, had skin that was darker than her own, was taunted by children in the street, but she makes no mention of having been racially abused in London herself.

She returned to Jamaica in 1825. Her first job when she came home was to nurse her 'old indulgent patroness', and she only returned to the family home when the elderly woman died. She then worked alongside her mother in the hotel and the 'medical' practice, sometimes helping with the troops at the British Army hospital at Up-Park Camp. In her autobiography she records how much she learned from her connections with the military:

> I had gained a reputation as a skilful nurse and doctress, and my house was always full of invalid officers and their wives from Newcastle or the adjacent Up-Park Camp. Sometimes I had a naval or military surgeon under my roof, from whom I never failed to glean instruction, given, when they learned my love for their profession, with a readiness and kindness I am never likely to forget.

In 1836 she married Edwin Horatio Hamilton Seacole. There's no real evidence to show what was claimed by his family and more than hinted at in his names – that he was the illegitimate son of Horatio Nelson and his mistress, Emma Hamilton. The story went that he'd been adopted by a 'surgeon, apothecary and man midwife' and in her will Mary left a ring to her friend, Lord Rokeby, claiming that it had been left to her late husband by his 'godfather', Viscount Nelson. There's no mention of the ring in Nelson's will.

The newly married couple opened a provisions store which did not do well and eventually they moved back to her mother's hotel at Blundell Hall. The marriage did not last long, as her husband seems to have had a very weak constitution. Indeed he occupies only a few lines in the first chapter of Mary's memoir. He died in 1844, soon after her mother's hotel had burned to the ground and been replaced by New Blundell Hall. Her mother's death followed quickly and Mary wrote that her grief was so great she did not stir for days.

She recovered pretty quickly though, claiming that for hot-blooded Creoles 'the sharp edge of our grief wears down sooner than theirs who preserve an outward demeanour of calmness, and nurse their woe secretly in their hearts'. She took over the running of the hotel, threw herself into the work, turned down a number of proposals of marriage and entertained numerous European military visitors to New Blundell Hall.

When a cholera epidemic swept through Jamaica in 1850, killing some thirty-two thousand Jamaicans, she gained more nursing experience. Her theory as to the source of the disease demonstrates that she had some understanding of the way diseases can be spread: she believed the cholera had been brought to the island on a steamer from New Orleans. She understood that certain diseases were contagious, which suggests she did have a degree of knowledge of conventional medicine. She says in her book, 'I believe that the faculty have not yet come to the conclusion that cholera is contagious, and I am not presumptuous enough to forestall them; but my people have always considered it to be so.'

In 1850 Mary's half-brother moved to Panama to establish a hotel and the following year she followed him there. Her arrival coincided with another cholera epidemic and her experience of treating the disease in Jamaica made her confident that she had the nursing skills to do useful work. She treated the first patient, who survived, and, as her reputation spread, sufferers flooded to her door. She treated the poor without charge, but the rich were expected to pay. Whether her treatments were free or not she was not terribly successful and lost a lot of her patients.

The medicines she used were mustard rubs, laxatives and lead acetate, and she attempted rehydration with water boiled with cinnamon. She records in her autobiography that she had moderate success and claims to have done better than 'a timid little dentist' who offered the only other medical treatment. He was a doctor sent by the Roman Catholic Church and didn't have much experience. Seacole admitted to 'lamentable blunders' in her remedies, which were different for each patient.

She claimed, though, to have learned valuable information about cholera after carrying out a post-mortem on an orphan child she had cared for. Quite what she learned from the child's corpse is unclear, but she did begin to insist that cleanliness, hydration, nutrition and ventilation were important in recovery. 'By my directions, doors and shutters were open, fires were lighted, and every effort was made to ventilate the place.' Towards the end of the epidemic, she caught the disease, nursed herself through it and survived, quickly moving on to her next business plan – the setting up of the British Hotel with the facilities for serving dinner to some fifty diners.

It was during a dinner to mark her intention to leave Panama that she records an example of out-and-out racism directed at her. A white American among the guests made a speech in which he commended her for the work she had done, but said the assembled company should 'rejoice that she's so many shades removed from being entirely black. If we could bleach her by any means we would and thus make her acceptable in any company as she deserves to be.' Seacole responded, 'I don't altogether appreciate your friend's kind wishes with respect to my complexion. If it had been as dark as any nigger's, I should have been just as happy and just as useful, and as much respected by those whose respect I value.'

Back in Jamaica Seacole began to hear of the escalating war against Russia in the Crimea and she decided to travel to England to volunteer as a nurse. She described her intention in her autobiography as a desire 'to experience the pomp, pride, and circumstance of glorious war'.

Thousands of troops from the Russian Empire on the one side, and Britain, France, Sardinia and the Ottoman Empire on the other, gathered on the Crimean peninsula in the Black Sea. So serious was the death toll from conflict, cholera and dirty, under-staffed hospitals that Sidney Herbert, the Secretary of State for War, asked Florence Nightingale to recruit a group of nurses to care for the soldiers. They left for Turkey in October 1853.

Mary Seacole travelled to England and tried to join the second group of nurses recruited for the Crimea. In her account of her efforts to join – an application to the War Office and other government departments – she claims to have presented 'ample testimony' of her experience in nursing. In the official records there is only one such testimony, from a former medical officer of the West Granada Mining Company in which Mary had had business interests. She was rejected. Whether or not she was turned down on the grounds of her race is unclear, but her lack of hospital experience may have counted against her.

She made another attempt to be sent to the Crimea when she applied for charitable support from the Crimean Fund, which had been set up to raise money by public subscription to support the sick and wounded at the battlefield. Again she was refused.

In 1855 the experienced businesswoman decided to fall back on what she knew best: she would travel to the Crimea under her own steam and set up 'the British Hotel' near Balaclava, which she intended would be 'a mess table and comfortable quarters for sick and convalescent officers'. In January 1855 she left on a Dutch ship, *Hollander*, travelling to Constantinople. During a stopover in Malta, Seacole met a doctor who had been working in Scutari where Nightingale was based, and he wrote Mary a letter of introduction.

The two women met at the Barrack Hospital in Scutari and Seacole records in her memoir that she was given a bed for the night and that Nightingale was friendly, offering whatever assistance Seacole might need. There's no evidence the two ever met again and a letter written by Nightingale to her brother-in-law, Sir Harry Verney, in the 1870s, suggests Florence had no desire to meet Mother Seacole, nor have her consort with the Nightingale nurses. She accused Mary of keeping a 'bad house' in Crimea and being responsible for 'much drunkenness and improper conduct'.

Seacole was nothing if not resourceful. She built her hotel from discarded metal and wood with the help of local labour and positioned it near the British supply route from Balaclava to the British camp near Sebastopol. It cost her £800 to build and her provisions came from London, Constantinople and the locality. She had two assistants who helped her with the cooking.

The business proved profitable and her efforts were praised by William Howard Russell, the special correspondent of *The Times*: '[Mrs Seacole] doctors and cures all manner of men with extraordinary success. She is always in attendance at the battlefield to aid the wounded, and has earned many a poor fellow's blessings.'

The Treaty of Paris, which ended the war, was signed in March 1856. As the soldiers left the battlefield, Seacole's business hit problems. Goods were still coming in which needed to be paid for – one guest had, in the past, been served champagne – and she was forced to auction most of her possessions at a loss. She left the Crimea together with the last of the troops, leaving Balaclava 'conspicuous in the foreground . . . dressed in a plaid riding habit, returning to England poorer than she left it'.

Mary arrived in London destitute and with failing health. She was declared bankrupt in November 1856, but she was saved by her reputation in the Crimea as remembered by the soldiers she'd served. The press wrote about her reduced circumstances and a charitable fund attracted contributions from a number of prominent people, saving her from financial ruin.

Her memoir was published in 1857 with a dedication by Russell, *The Times*' war correspondent, who wrote, 'I have witnessed her devotion and her courage . . . and I trust that England will never forget one who has nursed her sick, who sought out her wounded to aid and succour them, and who performed the last offices for some of her illustrious dead.'

During her final years, after one further trip to Jamaica, Mary Seacole stayed in London and became something of a minor celebrity. She was kept afloat financially by charitable donations and operated close to the Royal Family. One of her customers in the Crimea had been Prince Victor of Hohenlohe-Langenburg, a nephew of Queen Victoria. He carved the marble bust of her that was shown in the Royal Academy exhibition in 1872. It was through him that her skills were made known at court, particularly when the Princess of Wales discovered she could do a mean massage.

Mary Seacole died in Paddington in 1881, leaving an estate of more than £2,500. There was an obituary in *The Times* and she was buried in St Mary's Roman Catholic Cemetery in Kensal Green.

It's difficult to know how much of Seacole's history can be assumed to be true, given so much of it comes from the memoir where she describes herself as wonderful. She wore medals, including the British Crimea Medal and the French Légion d'honneur, but there's no record of her being awarded such honours. Some have speculated that she may simply have bought miniature medals herself.

Professor Lynn McDonald, editor of *The Collected Works of Florence Nightingale*, is, unsurprisingly, no great fan of Seacole's, although even she could not deny that this extraordinary woman had made a significant contribution to Britain's history. She wrote:

Mary Seacole, although never the 'black British nurse' she is claimed to have been, was a successful mixed-race immigrant to Britain. She led an adventurous life, and her memoir of 1857 is still a lively read. She was kind and generous. She made friends of her customers, army and navy officers, who came to her rescue with a fund when she was declared bankrupt. While her cures have been vastly exaggerated, she doubtless did what she could to ease suffering, when no effective cures existed. In epidemics pre-Crimea, she said a comforting word to the dying and closed the eyes of the dead. During the Crimean War, probably her greatest kindness was to serve hot tea and lemonade to cold, suffering soldiers awaiting transport to hospital on the wharf at Balaclava. She deserves much credit for rising to the occasion, but her tea and lemonade did not save lives, pioneer nursing or advance health care.

It seems to me that that last point is unfair. I'm not convinced Florence Nightingale and her team were able to do much more than offer comfort and care at the height of the conflict, and Mary's humanitarian efforts are pretty incredible for a woman with no proper training or, most importantly, influential connections. The blue plaque at her address at 14 Soho Square in London honours her as 'Jamaican Nurse, Heroine of the Crimean War' and Salman Rushdie in his novel *The Satanic Verses* makes reference to her: 'See, here is Mary Seacole, who did as much in the Crimea as another magic-lamping Lady, but, being dark, could scarce be seen for the flame of Florence's candle.'

'The Analytical Engine weaves
algebraic patterns just as the Jacquard
loom weaves flowers and leaves.'

Ada Lovelace

# 10

# Ada Lovelace

## 1815–1852

Not many newborn babies have the kind of welcoming accolade young Ada Lovelace had:

> Is thy face like thy mother's, my fair child!
> Ada! sole daughter of my house and heart?
> When last I saw thy young blue eyes they smiled,
> And then we parted – not as now we part,
> But with a hope.

She was born Augusta Byron on 10 December 1815 at 13 Piccadilly Terrace, London, the only legitimate child of George Gordon Noel Byron, the sixth Baron Byron, who was something of a poet and a renowned libertine. His wife was Anne Isabella Noel Byron. Soon after her birth her parents separated, caused quite a scandal, and she became instantly famous in the opening lines of Canto Three of Lord Byron's narrative poem *Childe Harold's Pilgrimage*.

It was after Byron's shocking affair with the married Lady Caroline Lamb that he set his sights on her cousin, Anne Isabella Milbanke, who turned down his first proposal. She later accepted him and they were married at Seaham Hall in County Durham on 2 January 1815. She was regarded as a highly moral woman, intelligent and mathematically gifted; Byron had called her his 'Princess of Parallelograms'. She was also an heiress, and it's often been said that Byron was attracted more by her money than her maths or her morals.

The marriage was a disaster. There were rumours, often circulated by a jealous Lady Caroline, of domestic violence, adultery with a number of actresses, incest with his half-sister Augusta Leigh and of homosexual relationships. On 16 January 1816, Lady Byron left him, taking the five-week-old Ada with her. On 21 April Byron signed the deed of separation.

Ada was brought up by her mother, who had sole custody of the child, as Byron made no claim on her and never saw her again after the separation. He died in 1824 when Ada was just eight and she was only shown the family portrait of her father when she was twenty.

Lady Byron took care to keep Ada out of the public eye, but the mother and daughter did not have a close relationship. She was often left in the care of her grandmother, who was said to have adored her. In one letter to her mother Lady Byron referred to the child as 'it', saying, 'I talk to it for your satisfaction, not my own, and shall be very glad when you have it under your eye.' She did, though, as the standards of the time demanded, present herself publicly as a loving mother and often wrote anxious letters to her mother enquiring after the child's welfare. She asked her mother to keep the letters in case there 'were ever a dispute' over the custody of Ada. It was unusual for a separated wife to win custody and a neglectful mother would have risked losing her child.

Lady Byron did, though, ensure that her daughter followed her own interest in mathematics, engaging a series of tutors who would guide her in maths and science, including a celebrated mathematician, Augustus De Morgan. Her mother, evidently, was deeply opposed to the idea that her daughter might become a poet, obviously worried that the naughtier side of her genetic history might prevail!

Lady Byron made sure that a number of her friends kept a close eye on her daughter as she reached her teenage years, looking out for any signs of her father's moral debauchery. Ada called them the 'Furies' and complained to a correspondent that they used to 'exaggerate or invent' stories about her. However, Lady Byron's concerns were not altogether unfounded. In 1833 Ada had an affair with a tutor and tried to run away with him. The Furies brought her behaviour to the attention of her mother and they covered the incident up to prevent a scandal.

Ada had been a sickly child and was often ill. When she was eight she suffered from terrible headaches which damaged her sight and, as happened to so many children before the measles vaccination was discovered in the 1960s, she had a severe bout of the disease in June 1829. She was lucky to survive, but was so ill she had to stay in bed for nearly a year, and when she was finally able to get up she could only walk with crutches.

Despite being so incapacitated by her illness, Ada was able to study during her period of confinement in bed. She concentrated on maths and began to work out for herself how to design mechanical objects. It's not surprising, given the fact that she had been stuck in her bedroom for such a long time, that she decided she really wanted to be able to fly and planned to make her own flying machine – quite an ambition for a girl of only fourteen in an age when a hot-air balloon was the only way of getting off the ground.

First she made wings, working out what material would be best and observing the anatomy of birds to determine what the relationship between the wings and the body should be. She wrote a book, *Flyology*, illustrating some of her findings. She wrote that one piece of equipment she would need was a compass to 'cut across the country by the most direct route', and her final step was to decide that the flying machine would be powered by steam.

She was a good forty years ahead of the first steam-powered monoplane which made lift-off, a 'hop' and a safe landing, manned by its designer Félix du Temple, in 1874. Ada's plane remained at the design stage.

One of her mother's acquaintances, as we learned in an earlier chapter, was the scientist Mary Somerville. She became one of Ada's teachers and it was through her that Ada met the mathematician Charles Babbage at the age of seventeen. Babbage showed Ada his first mechanical calculating engine, called the Difference Engine, and the earliest machine to be classed as a computer. She attended lectures about the engine, examined the plans, made further studies in mathematics and began to teach the subject. She also began to move in the same social circle as Babbage, which included De Morgan, the Somervilles, Charles Dickens, Michael Faraday and Babbage's close friend the scientist and inventor Sir Charles Wheatstone.

Ada was presented at court when she was seventeen and was described as a 'popular belle of the season in part because of her brilliant mind'. She became a regular at court and in 1835 she married William, eighth Baron King. In 1838 he became Baron Lovelace and she, in a professional sense, Ada Lovelace.

The couple had three children, Byron, Anne Isabella and Ralph Gordon, and Ada was extremely ill after the birth of her daughter, falling victim to 'a tedious and suffering illness, which took months to cure'. Despite her recurrent ill health she seems to have inherited some of her father's sexual improprieties. During her marriage she was reputed to have had a number of affairs with other men and to have developed a passion for gambling. She formed a syndicate with some of her male friends and used her mathematical skills to try to work out a winning way with her bets. She failed and had to admit losses of thousands of pounds to her husband.

It was during her marriage that she was told by her mother that her father and his half-sister, Augusta Leigh, had had a child together, Elizabeth Medora Leigh. She wrote to her mother, 'I am not in the least astonished. In fact you merely confirm what I have for years and years felt scarcely a doubt about, but should have considered it most improper in me to hint to you that I in any way suspected.' She blamed Augusta Leigh for the incestuous relationship. 'I fear she is more inherently wicked than he ever was.'

Despite the fascinatingly racy nature of her private life, it's for her work that she earns her place in the history of Britain – as the first computer programmer. Babbage was impressed from the outset by Ada's intellect and analytical skills, calling her 'the Enchantress of Number'. Her tutor, De Morgan, in a letter to her mother said her skills with numbers could 'lead her to become an original mathematical investigator, perhaps of first-rate eminence'.

There's much dispute among scientific circles as to the importance and originality of her contribution, but what sets Ada apart from the rest is the almost undoubtedly genetic combination of art and science which led her to see how Babbage's second machine – the Analytical Engine – might be used for more than simply crunching numbers.

In 1843 she published a translation from the French of an article on the Analytical Engine by an Italian engineer, Luigi Menabrea, to which Ada added extensive notes of her own. The Notes included the first published description of a stepwise sequence of operations – an algorithm – for solving certain mathematical problems, hence her designation as 'the first computer programmer'. The machine was never completed in her lifetime so her program was never tested.

But for me, the most telling aspect of Ada's genius is that she combines those two disciplines so often considered incompatible – art and science. She wrote that 'the Analytical Engine weaves algebraic patterns just as the Jacquard loom weaves flowers and leaves'. Her ideas were visionary, and it's clear there was a poetic bent to her thinking. She speculated that the Babbage

Engine 'might act upon other things besides number . . . the engine might compose elaborate and scientific pieces of music of any degree of complexity or extent'.

According to researchers at the Computer History Museum in California, it's here that her true talent and originality lie:

> The idea of a machine that could manipulate symbols in accordance with rules and that number could represent entities other than quantity mark the fundamental transition from calculation to computation. Ada was the first to explicitly articulate this notion and in this she appears to have seen further than Babbage. She has been referred to as 'the prophet of the computer age'. Certainly she was the first to express the potential for computers outside mathematics. In this the tribute is well-founded.

She was, though, dismissive of the idea of artificial intelligence. She wrote that 'The Analytical Engine has no pretensions whatever to *originate* anything. It can do *whatever we know how to order it to perform*. It can follow analysis; but it has no power of anticipating analytical relations or truths.' It remains to be seen whether or not she was right about that!

After Ada completed her work with Babbage she embarked on a variety of other projects. She was particularly interested in the brain and what might make a person mad. There was, of course, some family history here. Her father has gone down in history as being, in the words of Lady Caroline Lamb, 'mad, bad and dangerous to know', and both she and her mother were afraid that Ada may well have inherited his less attractive traits. She wrote about her plans to create a mathematical formula for how the brain gives rise to thoughts and nerves to feelings. She carried out research into electricity and its impact on the brain with the electrical engineer Andrew Crosse, and wrote about magnetism and the relationship between maths and music. Illness meant none of these projects were ever completed.

Ada Lovelace died tragically young at the age of thirty-six in November 1852; it's believed she had uterine cancer. Curiously, her father had died at exactly the same age. She had been in a lot of pain for several months, although she did manage to pose for a painting by Henry Phillips, whose father had painted Lord Byron.

Her mother took complete control of her life during her illness, excluding all her friends and confidantes from her bedside. Lady Byron persuaded her daughter to embrace religion, repent her 'Byronic' conduct and make her mother her executor. A couple of months before her death she is known to have made some sort of confession to her husband, which caused him to abandon her, but it is not known what she told him. She asked to be buried alongside her father at the Church of St Mary Magdalene in Hucknall, Nottinghamshire.

Ada is remembered in the twenty-first century and held up frequently as a model for other young women who are interested in science. A computer program created for the United States Department of Defense is called Ada in her memory, and London's Crossrail project even has a tunnel-boring machine known as Ada. Since 1998 the British Computer Society has awarded a medal in her name and in 2008 they began an annual competition for women who are studying computer science. A yearly conference for women undergraduates is called the BCSWomen Lovelace Colloquium and Ada Lovelace Day is an annual event held in October with the aim of raising 'the profile of women in science, technology, engineering and maths and to create new role models for girls and women'.

In 2015 the Computer History Museum opened an exhibition, 'Thinking Big: Ada Countess of Lovelace', to mark the two hundredth anniversary of her birth. Kirsten Taschev, vice president of exhibitions and collections, said of her: 'Ada Lovelace is often recognised for her partnership with Charles Babbage, but she was also a woman of fierce originality and intellectual interests. She envisioned the future of computers as symbol manipulators as well as their far-reaching creative possibilities. CHM's new exhibit uniquely explores both sides of Lovelace: the mathematician and the visionary.' I like to think Ada Lovelace is the ultimate confluence of art and science, genetically programmed to be her father's and her mother's daughter – a poet and a computer buff.

'The first thing women must learn is to dress
like ladies and behave like gentlemen.'

Elizabeth Garrett Anderson

# 11

# Elizabeth Garrett Anderson

## 1836–1917

As far as medicine goes, I've chosen Elizabeth Garrett Anderson as the first woman to qualify as a medical doctor in Britain because she did so as a woman, went on to specialise in women and children, and worked hard for the greater emancipation of women throughout her long life.

She was not, though, strictly the first. James Miranda Stuart Barry, who is thought to have entered this world in 1789 and lived until 1865, was actually born Margaret Anne Bulkley and qualified more than fifty years before Garrett Anderson. Bulkley chose to disguise herself as a man in order to gain acceptance to the medical school in Edinburgh. She lived the rest of her life as a man, working as a military surgeon, serving in India and in Cape Town, South Africa, where there is a museum dedicated to her/his achievements, one of which was the first Caesarean carried out in Africa where both the mother and child survived.

Barry died in England from dysentery and the woman who cared for him and dealt with the body reported to the authorities, after the funeral, that she had examined his anatomy and that she had discovered Inspector General Dr James Barry to be, in fact, female, and the stretch marks on his stomach indicated that he had, at some time, given birth to a child. The subterfuge came to light in an exchange of letters between George Graham of the

General Register Office and Major D. R. McKinnon, the doctor who had issued the death certificate on which Barry was identified as male.

McKinnon in his letter said that it was none of his business whether Dr Barry was a male or a female. He said he could only positively swear that the identity of the body was that of a person with whom he had been acquainted as Inspector General of Hospitals for a period of years. She certainly deserves an acknowledgement in this collection.

Elizabeth Garrett was born in Whitechapel in London and was the second of the nine children of Newson Garrett and his wife, Louisa. The family became well-to-do as the children grew up. Garrett was a self-made man who started out as a pawnbroker and developed a business as a grain merchant and maltster, operating out of Aldeburgh in Suffolk, which is where Elizabeth spent most of her childhood.

She was educated by her mother, then by a governess at home before attending, for five years from 1849, a boarding school for ladies at Blackheath in Kent run by the aunts of the poet Robert Browning. It was during this period that she met Emily Davies, who would later found Girton College, the first Cambridge college for women. The two of them became active members of the Langham Place circle and agreed on the careers they would pursue as part of their determined campaign to forward the advancement of women's rights and professional opportunities. Garrett would open the medical profession to women and Davies planned to open the doors of British universities.

The Langham Place Ladies were a group of middle-class, highly educated women who were associated with the Society for Promoting the Employment of Women and the *English Woman's Journal*. I think of them often when I arrive for work at Broadcasting House, around the corner from Langham Place. They were the foundation of the growing Victorian women's movement. As a result of her activities with the 'ladies' Garrett met Dr Elizabeth Blackwell, an Englishwoman who had been raised in the United States where she had, despite endless barriers placed in her way, managed to study medicine and obtain a degree.

Blackwell had come to London to have her name entered on the General Medical Council's newly established register. There was a temporary provision for doctors who qualified overseas to be registered after the Medical Act of 1858 and Blackwell was then, for a short time, the only woman on the list. During her visit she promoted the cause of women who wanted to enter the medical profession. Garrett was inspired.

Her father took some persuading that this was a suitable plan for a daughter of his. Mr Garrett had been a supporter of the education of his girls, but he was also a man deeply steeped in Victorian values. A respectable daughter with a good marriage was the aim of every responsible father, and the thought of his girl being involved in work that would have involved blood, guts and the more intimate parts of the human anatomy must have horrified him.

With Blackwell's support, Elizabeth managed to win him round to the extent that he agreed to give her his full support with both connections and finance. She was then able to begin her attempts to overcome the difficulties of prejudice against women she knew she would face. The profession was entirely dominated by men who, like her father, would have found the idea of a woman wielding a scalpel or discussing personal matters with a sick patient utterly unacceptable.

She made formal applications to several London teaching hospitals and to Edinburgh and St Andrews. She was turned down as a student by all of them, although Middlesex Hospital offered her a trial period from 1860 to 1861. She was to work as a nurse, but be given access to the operating theatre and classes on materia medica (medicine), Latin and Greek with the hospital's apothecary.

Eventually she was allowed into the dissecting room, but this seems to have proved too much for her shocked male colleagues. In 1861 they presented a memo to the hospital's medical school authorities making clear their determination that a woman should not be allowed admittance as a fellow student. They argued that the work they were expected to do with patients, cadavers and in the laboratory was simply not suitable for feminine sensibilities. Elizabeth was also an attractive young woman, modestly dressed in the style of the day with her hair neatly tied up in a bun, but her erstwhile colleagues were not happy with the distraction that the female of the species presented. What's more likely is that they were jealous of her academic and practical abilities.

The hospital excluded her from any further study there. But this was a woman who was described in her youth as being of indomitable will, unprepared to suffer fools gladly. She threatened legal action and the Society of Apothecaries, responsible for issuing medical licences, acknowledged that they could not prevent her from taking their examinations as long as she completed the required courses of study. This she had to do as a private student of teachers from recognised medical schools and after serving an apprenticeship under a licensed apothecary.

Happily, her wealthy, determined and by now encouraging father financed her and, in 1865, she obtained the licence of the Society of Apothecaries, which entitled her to have her name on the medical register. Only three of the seven applicants who took the exam passed it and Elizabeth gained the top marks. No wonder those young men were jealous and resentful. Soon after, the Society decided that no more women would be allowed to register, so Elizabeth was the first woman qualified in Britain to achieve such official status and the last until the Medical Act of 1876 allowed the British medical authorities to license all qualified applicants, regardless of gender.

*    *    *

In order to become a fully qualified doctor she had to leave the country and study at the University of Paris, and her low-status qualification as an apothecary was now raised to the level of MD. She was the first woman to achieve the degree, and in 1873 she was admitted to membership of the British Medical Association. In 1878 pressure was put on her to resign her membership as the BMA had voted against the admission of any more women. She refused and was the only female member for the next nineteen years, just one of several cases where Garrett would be the first woman to enter an all-male medical institution which would then block any further applications by women.

Now she was fully qualified to work as a doctor, Garrett set up her own practice in Upper Berkeley Street in London, just around the corner from fashionable Harley Street and only a few minutes' walk from Langham Place where the 'ladies' had congregated. She also set up the St Mary's Dispensary for Women and Children in Marylebone and, for this project, being well-connected among London's wealthy proved a great help. Charitable funds were found for the dispensary itself, as well as money to pay the fees for women who could not afford their own treatment.

Elizabeth had, for obvious reasons, a keen interest in education and in 1870 she stood as a candidate for the London School Board, the first time women had been allowed to stand. Robert Browning was an active supporter, as were a number of husbands of her more wealthy and influential patients. She won the highest number of votes in the whole of the capital.

James George Skelton Anderson was chairman of her election campaign. He worked for the Orient Steamship Line and was a son of a clergyman. The two married in 1871 and she went on to have three children, first a son, Alan, and two daughters, Margaret and Louisa. Margaret died of meningitis in 1875. All her children had the name Garrett Anderson, the name by which Elizabeth was known after her marriage. It was a rare move in the period for a married woman to insist that her own family name should continue down her line. Her younger sister, Millicent Garrett, a leading suffragist, did the same thing, becoming Millicent Garrett Fawcett – more of her in the next chapter.

Elizabeth carried on working hard after marriage and mother-hood, becoming a model for the mother who also wants to have a career, although she did resign an honorary post at the East London Hospital for Children, which she'd held since 1870, and she quit the school board. I guess even with the funds to pay for adequate childcare it wasn't absolutely possible to have it all! She once said, 'A doctor leads two lives, the professional and the private, and the boundaries between the two are never traversed.'

Her creation of the first hospital dedicated to the health of women with only female medical staff to care for them occurred in 1871, the same year as her wedding. The New Hospital for Women began as just ten beds above the dispensary, and the doctors she appointed were unregistered as they had medical degrees obtained abroad.

It was around this time that Elizabeth began to enter into the political arena on behalf of the burgeoning feminist movement. In 1874 Henry Maudsley (now known for his hospital in south London and his work in mental health) wrote an article on 'Sex and Mind in Education' in which he argued that education for women caused overexertion, and thus reduced their reproductive capacity, sometimes causing 'nervous and even mental disorders'. Elizabeth countered his argument by saying the real danger to women's mental health was not their education, but boredom. She said fresh air and exercise were infinitely preferable to sitting by the fire reading a novel.

It was in the same year, 1874, that she became a joint founder of the London School of Medicine for Women together with another medical pioneer, Sophia Jex-Blake. Elizabeth became a lecturer in the only medical school available to women and was Dean of the school from 1883 to 1902. She gave her students access to patients in the hospital, set them an example of female professionalism and always told them that 'the first thing women must learn is to dress like ladies and behave like gentlemen'. The school was later renamed the Royal Free Hospital of Medicine and prepared students for London University's medical degree, which was open to women from 1878.

In 1872 the New Hospital for Women moved to larger premises and then, in 1874, to a purpose-built facility on Euston Road. In 1918, the year after her death, it was named the Elizabeth Garrett Anderson and Obstetric Hospital and continued to employ only women doctors until it was absorbed into University College Hospital in the 1980s. It had been under threat of complete closure since the 1960s, but, when closure was announced by Camden Health Authority, the building was occupied in protest by the staff. The campaign to keep the hospital open continued until 1979. There is still an Elizabeth Garrett Anderson wing at UCH's new building, serving maternity and neonatal cases since 2008, but both male and female medical staff are employed.

By 1880 Garrett Anderson had set up a successful private practice alongside her work for poorer women and, in insisting that she would have only women caring for other women, she was able to conform to some degree to those Victorian standards of modesty that had threatened to block her advancement earlier in her career. Mind you, even today there are lots of women who would prefer to deal with a doctor of their own sex, particularly if their medical problems are obstetric or gynaecological. I remember a great sense of disappointment among my acquaintances – all in the midst of our childbearing years – when the principle she had established of women treating women was lost.

In addition to her clinical work, Garrett Anderson also became a surgeon – unusual for a woman even today – much to the horror of the management board of the hospital, who refused to allow major surgery to be performed on the premises. She went ahead and successfully removed a patient's diseased ovary – a very dangerous operation at the time. She wrote a short medical text-book, *The Student's Pocket Index*, in 1878, sharing the experience that she felt needed to be passed on to other young women entering the profession. She also contributed numerous articles on cases to the *British Medical Journal* and wrote for newspapers on medical matters and the women's cause.

In 1902, after a phenomenally successful career, Elizabeth and her husband moved back to the Garrett family home in Aldeburgh after the death of her mother. Her husband died five years later after suffering a stroke. She was pretty much retired from her medical work – she had resigned as senior physician at the New Hospital in 1892, only remaining as a consultant, but she did stand as mayor of Aldeburgh in 1908 and was elected. Thus she achieved another first – no other woman had ever succeeded in becoming a mayor in Britain.

Her two-year stint as mayor gave her an opportunity to pursue her interests in housing and sanitation, knowing that one of the most vital ways of improving the health of the population was to ensure that there was a substantial roof over the head of every family and that cleanliness would help keep infection and disease at bay. She was also a prime mover in the women's suffrage movement. She had begun her campaigning for women to have the vote in 1866 when she and Emily Davies gathered more than 1,500 on a petition asking that female heads of households should have the right to vote. She joined the first British Women's Suffrage Committee and became a member, in 1889, of the Central Committee of the National Society for Women's Suffrage.

After her husband's death, Elizabeth became even more active. She shocked some of Aldeburgh's town councillors by becoming, in 1908, a supporter of Emmeline Pankhurst's Women's Social and Political Union (WSPU), the more radical wing of the campaign, although in 1912 she stepped back from women who believed active revolution was the best way forward and publicly rejected the militant tactics of the suffragettes. She now leaned towards the suffragists' approach, led by her sister, Millicent Garrett Fawcett, believing that lobbying powerful men might be more effective. It was, in reality, an approach more suited to her character, which had always employed research, information and reasoned argument, rather than breaking windows or tying oneself to the railings of Parliament. Her daughter Louisa, on the other hand, who also became a doctor, joined the militant suffragettes and was imprisoned in 1912 for her activities.

Dr Elizabeth Garrett Anderson died in 1917 after a long illness and was consequently denied the opportunity of ever marking a ballot paper with a cross. The Great War was coming to a close and the following year, 1918, would see the Representation of the People Act in which limited suffrage was won for women of property over the age of thirty. It would take another ten years for universal suffrage to be achieved for all men and women over the age of twenty-one in the Equal Franchise Act of 1928.

Elizabeth is buried in the churchyard of St Peter and St Paul's Church in Aldeburgh, and I just wish I could tell her that in 2016 sixty per cent of all medical students are female. They have a great deal for which to thank her.

'I cannot say I became a suffragist. I always was one, from the time I was old enough to think at all about the principles of Representative Government.'

Millicent Garrett Fawcett

# 12

# Millicent Garrett Fawcett

## 1847–1929

I've often wondered whether, had I been around before women won the vote, I would have been a militant suffragette or a suffragist, relying on my capacity for reasoned argument and lobbying those powerful men in Parliament whose support would be necessary to get the law changed. Although I've been the President of the Fawcett Society – now the only organisation in Britain to work consistently for equality between men and women – since 2003, I suspect I may have been so angry and anxious for a speedy fulfilment of the demand for No Taxation without Representation that I may well have smashed a window or two, burned a post box and chained myself to the railings.

That was not Millicent Fawcett's way. Like her sister Elizabeth she spent her childhood in Aldeburgh in Suffolk, where she had been born. The Garretts were a close and loving family where the children were encouraged to learn, get plenty of physical exercise, read and sit around the dinner table for conversation and discussion. Their father, Newson, had been a Conservative politically, but he became a convert to Liberalism and the family was fervently interested in political debate.

Like her older sister, Milly attended the school in Blackheath, Kent from eleven, leaving at fifteen with a passion for literature, the arts and further education. Through Elizabeth and Louisa, the older sister who died young at the age of only thirty-two, she got to know the Langham Place Ladies and learned about the embryonic women's movement and its supporters.

She heard John Stuart Mill speak and was present when Garrett Anderson and Emily Davies organised the 1866 petition for women's suffrage. It called for 'the representation of all house-holders, without distinction of sex, who possess such property or rental qualifications as your honourable House may determine'. The two older women would not allow her to sign it. At the age of only nineteen they considered her too young, but they made no objection to her expending a huge amount of energy persuading others to sign it. There were 1,499 signatures on the petition when it was presented to Parliament by Mill. It failed.

It was, though, the start of Millicent's lifelong devotion to the cause of winning the vote for women. She was supported and encouraged by the friends she met through her sister and, of course, Elizabeth's struggles to qualify as a doctor naturally fired her little sister's enthusiasm for emancipation. It's said that, even as a teenager, Milly was identified as a possible leader of the suffrage movement and she later said of herself, 'I cannot say I became a suffragist. I always was one, from the time I was old enough to think at all about the principles of Representative Government.'

Milly married very young. She was eighteen when she met Henry Fawcett at a party held by a group of keen suffragists, and they married two years later. He was fourteen years her senior, a Professor of Political Economy at Cambridge and a Liberal MP. He had been with John Stuart Mill when the 1866 petition was presented to Parliament.

Millicent Fawcett described their marriage as having 'perfect intellectual sympathy'. They shared their politics, also had compatible interests in walking, rowing, riding and skating, and shared a sense of humour. A year after their marriage their first and only child, Philippa, was born.

The marriage was an extremely happy one. Henry was blind and, as Millicent acted as her husband's eyes, he was able to open political doors for her, introducing her to the men she would need to lobby if her aims were to be achieved. Henry supported her completely. Without such a sympathetic husband she would not have been able to run their houses in Cambridge and London, care for a new baby, write articles, act as his secretary, speak in public for the suffragist cause and be an active member of the Women's Suffrage Committee.

Henry Fawcett encouraged his wife to write, in addition to all her other activities. She managed to pen two novels, publish two works on classical economics and write the introduction to a new edition of Mary Wollstonecraft's great work, *A Vindication of the Rights of Woman*, although the Victorian version slipped up and replaced 'Woman' with 'Women'! I've never quite understood why such an active campaigner for women, on the cover of the new edition, is named as Mrs Henry Fawcett. It was the common way to address a married woman at the time, but one she rarely used. She was always Millicent Garrett Fawcett.

Being at the forefront of a controversial national campaign was not a recipe for an easy life. I haven't seen pictures of Milly wearing anything but a traditional Victorian woman's outfit with a high neck and full skirt. But she was leading a revolution where women walked the streets or rode their bicycles (shock, horror!) in the newfangled 'Rational Dress', which allowed some ease of movement and less corseted restriction. Some women were even courageous enough to wear a banner demanding 'Votes for Women' across the chest.

*Punch* cartoonists had a field day. They began to publish a torrent of abusive cartoons lampooning the suffrage cause; the magazine seemed to represent the view not only of comic artists and politicians but the majority of the British public as well. Millicent made lots of attempts to avert disapproval by her respectable behaviour and her clever, well-informed speeches, and she steadfastly refused to be put off by the widely held view that achieving the aims of the women's movement would be fraught with difficulties and would take a very long time. She chose to dismiss the strength of the opposition they faced and never wavered in her determination to promote the cause.

In 1997 Shelagh Diplock, a former director of the Fawcett Society, described Millicent as a formidable, if never a particularly charismatic, speaker:

> Millicent Garrett Fawcett, at the age of twenty-two, set out on the first speaking tour of her sixty-year-long campaign for women's suffrage. She would list the many reasons given why women should not be given the vote. It was said that women were intellectually inferior. They were physically inferior. They were too pure to be involved in politics. If given the vote, they would neglect their families and homes. Men would no longer open doors for them. Women did not really want the vote and so on. Then, one by one, she would demolish these points using her sharp logical mind and quick wit. This powerful mix of reasoned arguments to promote a cause, combined with humour to keep an audience listening, remains a most effective strategy to this day.

The Women's Suffrage Committee soon became the London Society for Women's Suffrage as other groups around the country, in Edinburgh and Manchester, began to be formed. They had all been heartened by the fact that Millicent's petition had at least been seen in Parliament: 'For the first step forward had been taken, the challenge had been thrown down, and the Cause had been advanced into the political lists.' But their belief that the cause would be popular simply because it was just was misguided.

Nevertheless, the movement grew. There were numerous strong and resourceful women who were prepared to endure the ridicule they faced in standing up for women's rights, and there were a number of men who also proved essential to the movement. Always positioned at the front of her armies of supporters was Millicent Garrett Fawcett. She served on the board of most of the suffrage organisations, spoke on platforms, wrote and lobbied.

There were endless difficulties and debates about where the women's campaigning energies should be concentrated. As we've seen in the previous chapter, medicine and education were the preoccupations of Elizabeth Garrett Anderson and Emily Davies, but for young Millicent, the vote was the main focus and she was continually aware of the need to avoid the racier side of the campaign and remain the calm, informed lobbyist who had to persuade rather than alienate the powerful men whose minds she wanted to change.

As a consequence of the need to present a respectable front, Milly was forced to back down from a campaign she would have dearly loved to support. Josephine Butler was a fellow feminist and social reformer who, between 1869 and 1886, worked to have the Contagious Diseases Act repealed. The Act required that any woman suspected of being a prostitute must be examined for venereal infection. If she were found to have the disease she would be locked in hospital until she was cured. If she refused to submit to a genital examination she could be given a prison sentence of up to three months.

Milly agreed with Butler that it was unjust that prostitutes, or indeed any woman suspected or accused of being one, should be examined regularly for venereal disease when the men who bought their bodies were not subjected to such demands. But Butler's efforts were widely considered unsuitable for a woman of modest Victorian conduct. Millicent was keen that she should not be associated with the 'violent opposition' the Butler campaign aroused and supported her only in private.

As the century wore on and further attempts were made by sympathetic MPs to bring forward a Bill or resolution to advance the cause of suffrage, the tone of the response in the House was said to be not so much hostile as facetious. The women's reasoned arguments and demands were simply not taken seriously, even in Parliament.

In 1884 Henry Fawcett died suddenly, leaving Millicent a widow at the age of only thirty-seven. Her naturally reticent nature prevented any outpouring of emotion, but those close to her commented on how deeply she grieved for him. She never considered marrying again.

Millicent sold the houses in Cambridge and London and moved with Philippa and one of her sisters, Agnes, into 2 Gower Street in Bloomsbury, where a blue plaque now honours her memory. She was not short of money. Her sister was a successful businesswoman who ran a home improvement company and Millicent made a living from her writing. She made regular contributions to the *Contemporary Review* and wrote a number of biographies, including *Some Eminent Women of Our Times* and *The Life of Her Majesty Queen Victoria*.

She also became the suffrage movement's official leader, becoming the president in 1897 of the National Union of Women's Suffrage Societies (NUWSS) and adopting the suffragist colours of green, white and red (GWR) – the initials stood for 'Give Women Rights', and differed from the suffragettes' green, white and purple, symbolising hope, purity and dignity.

Not all of her views would play well with modern members of the society named after her, which, in 2016, celebrated its one hundred and fiftieth anniversary – the history of the Fawcett Society began at the time of the 1866 petition to Parliament presented by John Stuart Mill and Henry Fawcett.

Millicent supported compulsory primary education for young children, but believed parents should be expected to pay for it and be prevented from profiting from the earnings of their young. As a believer in the principle of family responsibility she opposed free school meals and later family allowances, and she was active in an unpopular campaign in the late 1880s for children to be banned from working in pantomime or in the theatre.

As a passionate believer in the free market, she had been a supporter of the National Union of Working Women and was concerned about the welfare of working-class women, but she did not approve of legislation to protect them. She felt that there should be no discriminatory legislation on the part of women that was not equally available to men.

She even caused controversy and was widely opposed when she questioned the case for intervention on the part of women whose faces had been horribly mutilated during the course of their work at Bryant and May's match factory in the East End of London. The condition was known as 'phossy jaw', as the necrosis was caused by the phosphorus used to make the matches. The social activist Annie Besant published an exposé in the magazine *The Link* describing the factory as a prison house and the girls as white slaves.

Besant encouraged and supported the girls during the Match Girls' Strike of 1888, which became an extremely significant moment in the history of the trade union movement. Bad employers were shamed in the press, the match girls, aided by Annie Besant, forced Bryant and May to agree to improve their conditions and a union, one of the first to represent women and a then rare example of a union for unskilled workers, was formed and would last until 1903. *The Link* described the strike as putting 'new heart into all who are struggling for liberty and justice'.

Millicent was aware of how badly women workers were paid compared to men and her major contribution to economic theory was an analysis of the inequality of women's wages. She wrote that it was an inevitable consequence of two things: the 'crowding' of women into a narrow range of jobs as a result of laws that restricted women's opportunities for employment, and discrimination against women perpetrated by the male trade union movement. She argued that it was counterproductive for women to demand equal pay for equal work because the labour market made it impossible for them to achieve equal work – an argument that's common even today when the fight for equal opportunity and equal pay goes on.

Millicent thought demanding more money might well persuade employers that it was hardly worth employing women at all if they ceased to be the cheaper option. She abandoned that argument when the range of jobs open to women was widened during the First World War, as men went to the front and women took up the jobs they had left behind to keep the country working.

In some ways, then, she was a rebel against her times, but she was also a woman of her time. She had statesmanlike qualities, which made her an important leader of the British women's movement, but her Victorian values are clear. She was a passionate believer in the British Empire and a severe opponent of Home Rule for Ireland and independence for India. She also became closely associated with the purity movement, prompted by the exposure of child prostitution by the newspaper editor W. T. Stead, who was a pioneer of investigative journalism. He arranged the purchase of a thirteen-year-old girl, Eliza Armstrong, to highlight the existence of the trade, and wrote a series of devastating articles about child exploitation in the *Pall Mall Gazette*. He was later imprisoned for three months, having been found guilty of failing to secure the permission of the girl's father for the purchase. The story inspired George Bernard Shaw to write *Pygmalion* and call his character Eliza.

Millicent was one of a number of women who joined the purity movement as a result and she campaigned for years, as a founder member of the National Vigilance Association, to protect girls from being trapped into prostitution, to curb child abuse by raising the age of consent, to make incest a criminal offence, to stamp out the 'white slave trade' and to make cruelty to children within the family illegal. She had some success. One of her most vociferous campaigns was to end the practice of excluding women from courtrooms when sexual offences were being considered.

She did tend to be rather censorious in a way that might not appeal to modern feminists, although she did, at least, insist that equality should dominate her moral arguments. By her moral code, neither men nor women were suitable for public office if they indulged in private immorality. She disapproved publicly of a friend who became pregnant before marriage and she tried to destroy the career of the Unionist MP Harry Cust. He was an unrepentant seducer, which, for Millicent, overrode his strong support for the suffragist cause. When some Edwardian feminists began to advocate 'free love' she was appalled and a copy of the *Freewoman*, which was sent to her, was torn up into small pieces and described as 'objectionable and mischievous'. So perhaps it's surprising that, when she gave evidence to the Gorell Commission on divorce in 1910, she argued in favour of divorce by consent.

As Britain moved into a new century, mass support for women's suffrage grew and even the passionately non-violent Millicent had to acknowledge that it was the militant campaign launched by the Pankhursts in 1905 that had really brought the movement to the attention of the nation. As the nineteenth century had come to a close, the NUWSS seemed to have made little progress towards the goal of winning votes for women. Letters of congratulation had been dispatched to their sisters in places like Australia and Wyoming, where women had achieved what the British campaigners had failed so spectacularly to win.

The National Union of Women's Suffrage Societies was re-organised under Millicent's presidency in 1907 and was by far the largest of the suffrage societies with more than fifty thousand members by 1913. It remained committed to constitutional reform. Through her close connections with the universities she attracted well-educated women into the leadership of the movement, which helped give credibility to the cause among educated men. She arranged demonstrations and marches in which she took the lead and in 1908 became the first woman to address the Oxford Union, although the Union did not vote in favour of votes for women until 1913.

Millicent worked hard to attract working-class women into the movement, to join the educated women who had already signed up, saying she believed in 'a grand freemasonry between different classes of women'. It's been suggested by the historian Janet Howarth that the law-abiding strategy of the NUWSS was more popular among working women than suffragette militancy.

As the direct action policy of the Pankhursts' WSPU stepped up there was growing tension between the suffragists and suffragettes. Millicent described this period as 'the most difficult time of my forty years of suffrage work'. She openly expressed her disapproval of the suffragettes' storming of Parliament in 1909, describing it as an 'immoral and dastardly thing to have done'. She was, though, determined that no war should be declared between the suffragists and the suffragettes. The individual suffragettes who made the headlines and were courageous enough to face imprisonment, hunger strikes and force-feeding won her admiration. In 1906 she had held a banquet at the Savoy in honour of the first ten suffragette prisoners, although she was criticised for it in the press and by those who considered the suffragettes' violent tactics to be illegal acts that deserved severe punishment.

The two sides of the movement split in 1912, when the acts of symbolic violence such as breaking windows escalated into arson and bombings. The suffragettes never killed or even injured anyone, but it was clear to Millicent that such acts were damaging to the cause. Still, she argued that the government was responsible for provoking women into breaking the law, while also declaring that the punishments meted out to them, such as long prison sentences and force-feeding, were excessive given the nature of their crimes. The tariff for length of sentence was, she said, more lenient for men, even if their crimes had been more heinous.

The First World War brought an end to activism in the suffrage cause, but Millicent held the NUWSS together by directing its members into war work and was admired by a wide range of politicians for her efforts. There were, though, some serious fallings-out with fellow suffragists who, conflating feminism with pacifism, objected to her wholehearted, patriotic support for the war effort. She saw the war as a necessary conflict that was defending free institutions against the militarism of Prussia.

In 1917 it became accepted that the franchise should be granted to all servicemen, which effectively meant universal suffrage for all adult males. Before the war only men over twenty-one who owned property had the right to vote. The 1918 Representation of the People Act extended the right to all men over twenty-one, regardless of wealth or class. An all-party speakers' conference held in 1917 was persuaded to recommend a limited right to vote for women.

There's no doubt the war and women's work in nursing, running the railways, driving ambulances and working in factories certainly contributed to the change of mind, but it's clear that pressure from Millicent, particularly in persuading Lloyd George to support her, was instrumental in the fight being won. She also persuaded her members to compromise and accept the limited enfranchisement on offer in 1918. She lobbied politicians to ensure the Bill passed through Parliament in 1918 and women over the age of thirty who owned property won the first step towards universal suffrage, which was finally achieved ten years later in 1928.

Millicent was now seventy-one and gave old age as her reason for resigning from the presidency of the NUWSS in 1919. It was rechristened the National Union of Societies for Equal Citizenship (NUSEC) and she remained associated with it for the last decade of her life. She was a vice president of the League of Nations Union, took part in campaigns to open up the legal profession and the civil service to women, fought for women to have equal access to divorce and continued to argue for equal suffrage.

During the Paris peace conference, she led a deputation that hoped to place women's suffrage on the agenda, and she was persuaded, as a result of women's war work, to begin to press for equal pay. She was, though, never persuaded by feminist contemporaries such as Eleanor Rathbone that family allowance was a good thing. She resigned from the NUSEC in 1925 when the union voted to press for family allowance. She never changed her attitudes to morality and imperialism, although she did say she approved of the change of fashion after the war, which freed women from restrictive corsets and shortened their skirts and their hair.

Millicent Garrett Fawcett has, I believe, been grossly underestimated in the story of the battle for votes for women. She was the most tireless campaigner for women to have equal rights as citizens and fought for us to have the right to education, work and freedom from exploitation and sexual abuse. In 1925 her efforts were recognised when she became Dame Millicent Garrett Fawcett. At the end of a long career, during which she never stopped working for her causes, she died after a short illness at her home in Gower Street in 1929. She was cremated at Golders Green and her memorial in Westminster Abbey, added in 1932 to the monument to her husband, says: 'She won citizenship for Women'.

'I am what you call a hooligan.'

Emmeline Pankhurst

# 13

# Emmeline Pankhurst

## 1858–1929

It's Emmeline Pankhurst's name that has long been most closely associated with the campaign for votes for women, although, I hope, after the preceding chapter on Millicent Garrett Fawcett, it will become clear that it was both the peaceful and persuasive suffragist movement combined with the militant, publicity-conscious tactics of Pankhurst's suffragettes that made the cause impossible to ignore.

Emmeline Pankhurst was born in Sloane Street in Moss Side, Manchester to Robert Goulden, who owned a calico printing and bleach works, and his wife, Sophia Jane Craine. I've always found it deliciously ironic that her mother was born on the Isle of Man. Emmeline was the eldest of ten children and, from an early age, had to do her bit to care for her younger siblings.

She was educated at home, learned to read when she was very young and it was her job to read the daily paper to her father while he ate his breakfast. An interest in politics was thus fostered at the table. Family history also taught her that protest was a necessary part of politics if you felt something passionately. Her paternal grandfather had taken part in the Peterloo demonstration for parliamentary reform and universal suffrage in 1819. A huge crowd of demonstrators gathered peacefully in what's now St Peter's Square in Manchester – between sixty and eighty thousand – and were set upon by a cavalry charge. Sabres were drawn and civilian blood shed in a defining moment of British history. The number killed is not altogether clear. Some sources say fifteen, others eighteen, but it's agreed that at least one woman and a child were among them. Some were killed by sabres, others by clubs or by being trampled to death by the horses. Some seven hundred lay injured. It became known as the Peterloo Massacre and so shocked a local businessman, John Edward Taylor, that he went on to help set up the *Manchester Guardian* newspaper. Mr Goulden senior was said to have narrowly missed death.

Emmeline's brothers called her 'the dictionary' because she had such a command of the English language. She spoke well, wrote well and they envied her perfect spelling. She is said to have been in bed one night, pretending to be asleep, when she heard her father say, 'What a pity she wasn't born a lad.'

She had learned for herself that girls' education was considered less important than that of boys when she was sent with her sister to a middle-class girls' school. She was appalled when she found little emphasis on reading, writing, arithmetic or any kind of intellectual pursuit there. A lot of her lessons were devoted to learning how to be the perfect housewife, making a home comfortable for a man. In her ghostwritten autobiography, *My Story*, published in 1914, she said, 'It was made quite clear that men considered themselves superior to women, and that women apparently acquiesced in that belief.'

When Emmeline began to be involved in active sexual politics she described herself as a 'conscious and confirmed suffragist'. She had been made aware, from when she was tiny, of the meaning of slavery and emancipation. When she was five she had been asked by her parents to collect pennies in a 'lucky bag' for the newly emancipated slaves in the United States. Both her parents were supporters of equal suffrage and Sophia Jane took the monthly *Woman's Suffrage Journal*, edited by Lydia Becker, one of

Manchester's foremost suffragists. When Emmeline was fourteen she asked her mother to take her to a meeting where Becker was speaking – she found the speaker's ideas most engaging.

It was around this time, in late 1872, that Emmeline was sent to study in Paris. Her closest friend was a girl whose father was a famous republican who was imprisoned in New Caledonia for his part in the Paris Commune. Emmeline became a confirmed Francophile and found his story and Thomas Carlyle's popular book *The French Revolution* an inspiration throughout her life. Carlyle's work seems to revel in the violence of the revolutionary terror and welcomes the destruction of the old order in French society. Emmeline would never go so far as to advocate the guillotine for those who opposed her; indeed her suffragettes would be encouraged to damage property without harming human life, but she had learned that change can be achieved by violent revolution.

When she returned to Manchester from France she was almost nineteen and expected by her mother to fall in line in the way a respectable young lady should. Emmeline was not one to waste her energies on boring household tasks and made her view plain to her mother on numerous occasions. There were constant rows between the two women, best illustrated by the afternoon when Mrs Goulden demanded that her daughter should go and fetch her brother's slippers and help make him comfortable. 'No way,' was Emmeline's response. 'If he wants his slippers he can go and get them himself. As for you, mother, if, as you claim, you are truly in favour of women's rights, you are certainly not showing it at home.'

Emmeline began to work with the women's suffrage movement and met a man who was a well-known radical lawyer and supporter of the women's cause. He was Dr Richard Marsden Pankhurst and, despite the twenty-year age gap, they fell in love and married in 1879.

Their four children, Christabel, Sylvia, Henry Francis (known as Frank) and Adela, were born in the first six years of their marriage and while Emmeline's involvement in public affairs was slowed down by motherhood, it far from stopped. In 1880 she was elected onto the committee of the Manchester National Society for Women's Suffrage and was asked to join the Married Women's Property Committee. She and her husband worked together closely on these committees and she campaigned twice on his behalf in 1883 and 1885 when he stood as an independent parliamentary candidate. They proposed the abolition of the House of Lords and the monarchy, adult suffrage on equal terms for both sexes, the disestablishment of the Church of England, nationalisation of land and Home Rule for Ireland. Pretty radical stuff! Pankhurst was not elected.

In 1886 the family left Manchester for London and set up home in Hampstead Road. Emmeline was keen to have financial independence and to support her husband materially so that he could concentrate on his politics, so she opened a shop selling fancy goods. There were frequent trips to Manchester on political business and it was during one of those visits that four-year-old Frank fell ill. When the parents arrived home he was critical. He had been wrongly diagnosed with croup, which turned out to be diphtheria, and he died in September 1888.

The cause of his illness may have been faulty drainage at the rear of the house in Hampstead, so the family closed the shop and moved to a rented house at 8 Russell Square. It was there that her fifth child was born. He was also called Henry Francis in memory of his older brother, but was known as Harry.

8 Russell Square became a centre for radical politics where Fabians – members of the Fabian Society, Britain's oldest political think tank, founded in 1884 to develop public policy on the left – anarchists, socialists and suffragists would meet. The Pankhursts developed a close friendship with the Scottish socialist Keir Hardie, who was elected to Parliament as an Independent MP for West Ham South in 1892. He helped form the Independent Labour

Party (ILP) the following year and in 1900 the Labour Party was born. Hardie was the first Labour Member of Parliament when he was elected that year as the junior member for the dual-member constituency of Merthyr Tydfil and Aberdare. He would represent the constituency for the rest of his life.

In 1893 the Pankhurst family went back to Manchester to 4 Buckingham Crescent. Emmeline resigned from the Women's Liberal Association to join the ILP and in 1894 she was elected as an ILP member to the Chorlton Board of Guardians. The work involved the inspection of workhouses and she was often horrified by the terrible conditions she found there, particularly where girls and single women with babies were concerned. She was described as compassionate and fearless, and managed to introduce a number of improvements.

Her first brush with the law came in 1896 when some of her fellow members of the ILP were sent to prison for giving political speeches in the open air at Boggart Hole Clough, a large urban park, which was owned by Manchester City Council. The Pankhursts and their children were all involved in speaking out in defence of free speech, often appearing in the Clough, and she would shout that she was prepared to go to prison herself. She was taken to court but the case against her was dismissed. Confronted by such opposition to her beliefs, and to her right to speak in public, Emmeline's association with the ILP grew even stronger. In 1897 she was elected to the party's National Administrative Council.

The following year her beloved husband died suddenly as a result of stomach ulcers. He was only sixty-two. His legal practice had never made much money because his close association with the socialist movement had made him an unpopular choice for a great many potential clients. Emmeline and the children were left to struggle financially, and she refused any charitable help from political friends and associates. Instead she asked that donations should be made to build a hall in her husband's memory in Salford.

Meanwhile, she moved the family to cheaper accommodation in 62 Nelson Street, which is now the home of the Pankhurst Centre, a small museum celebrating the birth of the suffragette movement. There was another failed attempt at opening a shop to earn money to keep the family from poverty and finally Emmeline accepted a salaried post as registrar of births and deaths in Chorlton. This work brought her into contact with working-class women who had come to register the births of their babies. They were often young, unmarried girls who had been abused by relatives or employers, and her determination that women must improve their position in society grew ever stronger.

It was five years after Richard's death that the Pankhurst Hall in Salford was finally opened as the headquarters for the local branch of the ILP. Only one problem. It had been decided that women would not be allowed to join the party there. Emmeline immediately left the ILP in protest at what she saw as a waste of her commitment and time to the socialist movement. She became convinced that the only solution for women was to found their own political party.

In her autobiography she wrote, 'It was in October, 1903, that I invited a number of women to my house in Nelson Street, Manchester, for the purposes of organisation. We voted to call our new society the Women's Social and Political Union.' It was agreed the organisation would be open to women of any class and its focus would be a campaign to win votes for women, with the motto 'Deeds not Words'. A few years later, in 1908, the WSPU adopted a colour scheme of purple, white and green, symbolising dignity, purity and hope.

The suffragettes were, from the beginning, adept at publicity and self-promotion, understanding the need for a slogan and an identifiable colour scheme. Money would be raised from the sale of scarves and hats in suffragette colours, and from postcards and booklets whose sense of humour often matched those of the *Punch* cartoons, but told the other side of the woman question. The suffragettes clearly showed the positive side of the emancipation of women, whereas the *Punch* cartoonists invariably portrayed it as a potential disaster for hearth and home.

The first notable campaign carried out by the WSPU, after a number of peaceful appearances at trade unions' conferences and street demonstrations, came in the autumn of 1905 on the eve of a general election, when it was expected the Liberals would win. Emmeline's oldest daughter, Christabel, and Annie Kenney, a working-class Manchester woman, went to a Liberal Party meeting at the Free Trade Hall (now a posh hotel) and asked a question: 'Will the Liberal government, if returned, give votes to women?' No one answered their question, so they asked it again. They were bundled out of the hall, charged with obstruction and sentenced to pay a fine or go to prison. Emmeline offered to pay their fines, but the two refused and were imprisoned for several days. It proved the turning point in the suffrage campaign. As a result of extensive newspaper coverage, Deeds not Words got noticed.

In 1907 the WSPU moved its headquarters to London and Emmeline left her job as registrar of births and deaths, her only source of income. She now had no settled home and lived in various rented flats, hotels or homes of friends, but was awarded a stipend of £200 per annum from WSPU funds.

Emmeline Pethick-Lawrence became treasurer of the organisation in 1906. She and her husband, Frederick, were wealthy business-people and she brought those skills and some personal money to the Union. Donations from supporters were often generous, and at some meetings, where the charismatic Mrs Pankhurst spoke, as much as £14,000 could be raised. Money, jewels and other valuables were frequently thrown onto the platform.

Emmeline Pankhurst's first experience of prison came early in 1908 when she led a deputation to the House of Commons and they were arrested for obstruction. She served a month in what was known as the second division, reserved for common criminal offenders, rather than the first division for political prisoners. Later that same year, in October, she was back in the dock in Bow Street, accused of incitement to disorder with Christabel and Flora Drummond – a WSPU organiser known as 'The General' because of the uniform she chose to wear. They had published a handbill encouraging a 'rush' on the House of Commons. The three women defended themselves in court. Emmeline's speech in her defence and her description in the dock of the miserable lives led by so many women moved people to tears. Nevertheless, she was sentenced to three months in jail.

Prison became a familiar home for suffragettes who had taken part in angry and impatient demonstrations. In 1909 members decided that they would go on hunger strike in an attempt to persuade the authorities that they should be treated not as common criminals but as *political* prisoners. Their demands were not met. Instead, force-feeding began where a tube would be pushed down a weak and hungry prisoner's throat and sustenance poured into the stomach, an extremely painful practice. Emmeline was horrified and condemned the government for torturing women who had merely expressed a justifiable grievance. The force-feeding continued, but, of course, publicity and sympathy came as a result.

Emmeline left for the United States in October that same year and was greeted enthusiastically wherever she spoke, particularly at Carnegie Hall in New York. She opened her speech with, 'I am what you call a hooligan.' She was a brilliant orator, always able to demonstrate the most important qualities for an effective speaker – 'Make 'em laugh, make 'em cry, make 'em think.'

Her triumphant conquering of America and Canada raised much-needed funds for the WSPU, but there was tragedy on her return. Her surviving son, Harry, had developed inflammation of the spinal cord, which had left him paralysed from the waist down. In January 1910 he died and Sylvia said her mother was broken emotionally by his death. She threw herself into the general election campaign of that year and followed the Union's policy of opposing all Liberal candidates, regardless of their attitude for or against the enfranchisement of women.

The Liberal government did win the election, but with a greatly reduced majority. The Liberals had 275 seats, the Conservatives 273, the Irish Nationalists 82 and Labour 40. A left-wing journalist, Henry Brailsford, who was sympathetic to the women's cause (he had resigned from his job at the *Daily News* because the paper had supported the force-feeding of suffragette hunger strikers) thought the make-up of a hung Parliament, with the balance of power held by Labour and the Irish, might offer a better opportunity for successful lobbying. He formed a Conciliation Committee for Women's Suffrage and for the time being Emmeline called a halt to militant action.

The committee came up with the Women's Franchise Bill. In order that the Conservatives should not be frightened off, its demands were narrow. It sought to extend the vote to independent female property owners, but would exclude women whose husbands met the property qualification. Very few women would have won the vote in those circumstances and Emmeline was opposed to the Bill in principle, but was furious when, after passing a Second Reading, it was opposed by the Home Secretary, David Lloyd George, and by the Prime Minister, Herbert Asquith.

When Parliament reassembled no reference was made to the Bill. The WSPU organised a deputation of protest to the House of Commons on 18 November. The police brutality on that day led to it being called Black Friday. Around 300 women joined the protest and 119 were arrested. Many protesters were attacked by the police and two women later died of their injuries. There were allegations of sexual assault against a number of officers, but none of them were pursued. Four days later Emmeline organised another march, this time to Downing Street. Among the 156 women arrested on that occasion were Emmeline and her sister, Mary. No evidence was offered against Emmeline so she avoided prison on this occasion, but Mary died at Christmas as a result of the injuries she had suffered at the hands of the police on Black Friday.

There was much toing and froing around a revised Conciliation Bill when the second 1910 election was announced for December of that year. The WSPU felt it could support the Bill now as it included all women householders. Militant action was again suspended and Emmeline made another speaking trip to North America. During her absence she discovered the Prime Minister had announced that a Manhood Suffrage Bill would be introduced in the next session that would broaden men's enfranchisement. He said it would allow an amendment for women. Such an amendment could not be carried without the support of the government, which Emmeline was convinced would not be forthcoming. She returned to London on 18 January 1912, according to Sylvia, speaking of 'Sedition!' and 'The Women's Revolution'.

In February 1912, at a meeting to welcome back newly released prisoners, Emmeline announced a new policy. She had decided that reasoned argument, speeches, demonstrations and chaining oneself to the railings of the House of Commons were getting them nowhere. Instead, the stone would serve as the weapon and replace the argument at the next demonstration. She had lessons in stone-throwing from the composer Ethel Smyth (more of her in the next chapter) and the WSPU struck for the first time, without warning, on 1 March, smashing windows in the West End of London.

Later that afternoon she and two other women broke windows in Downing Street and two more days of window-smashing followed. In court she argued that women had failed to get the vote because they had failed to employ the methods of disruption often used by men. She was sentenced to several months in prison, but released after a few days in order to attend a new trial with the Pethick-Lawrences, charged with conspiracy. Christabel had escaped to Paris.

Again Emmeline made political speeches from the dock, arguing that women had been driven to violence by the opposition of the government. The three defendants were found guilty and sentenced to nine months in the second division, with common criminals. They threatened hunger strike if they were not sent, as political prisoners, to the first division. Their demand was granted, but it was not extended to other suffrage prisoners. The three leaders joined the others in a mass hunger strike and again force-feeding began. Emmeline resisted the doctor and the warders when they came to her cell. When she picked up a heavy earthenware jug and threatened to defend herself if they came near her, they withdrew. She was released on medical grounds two days later and was never threatened with force-feeding again.

Emmeline spent some time travelling to see Christabel in France using the name Mrs Richards. She cut back on her speaking engagements and spent more time in London at WSPU's headquarters. There was a major rift between her and the Pethick-Lawrences: Emmeline was keen to increase the programme of militant action; the Pethick-Lawrences were not. Emmeline and Christabel told them, perhaps rather brutally given the unwavering support they had provided for so long, that their services were no longer required.

It was an unwise move in the long term. A number of WSPU members were furious that the couple had been so dismissed. Some of Emmeline's followers retained their faith in her leadership, but the WSPU lost a lot of its rich and influential supporters, and it now fell to her to take over the job of treasurer and fundraiser, the work that had been carried out so effectively by Mrs Pethick-Lawrence.

Mrs Pankhurst, with the revolutionary bit between her teeth, announced a new plan for militant action at a meeting at the

Royal Albert Hall on 17 October 1912. She emphasised that the WSPU would support no political party and that the 'revolution' would now include attacks on both public and private property. There must, she said, be no danger to human life, but that it was just to attack the things she considered were most valued by society – 'money, property and pleasure'. 'Militancy is right,' she concluded, 'because no measure worth having has been won in any other way.'

The militant action escalated with such tactics as setting fire to pillar boxes, raising false fire alarms, attacking works of art – Mary Richardson famously slashed Velázquez's *Rokeby Venus* in the National Gallery – severing telegraph and telephone wires, and damaging golf courses. No human life was put at risk during these activities, but there is one attack, which took place in 1913, where the suffragettes were extremely lucky that no one was killed or injured.

On 20 February *The Times* reported, 'An attempt was made yesterday morning to blow up the house which is being built for Mr. Lloyd George near Walton Heath Golf Links.' One device had exploded, causing some £500 worth of damage. Another had failed to go off. That evening, at a meeting in Cardiff, Mrs Pankhurst made a confession. 'We have blown up the Chancellor of the Exchequer's house . . . [F]or all that has been done in the past, I accept responsibility. That I have advised, I have incited, I have conspired.'

Lloyd George saw the action as an act of terrorism, as he told Sir George Riddell, the proprietor of the *News of the World*. Sir George wrote of the conversation in his diary.

L. G. much interested. Said the facts had not been brought out and that no proper point had been made of the fact that the bombs had been concealed in cupboards, which must have resulted in the death of twelve men had not the bomb which first exploded blown out the candle attached to the second bomb which had not been discovered, hidden away as it was.

The workmen had been due to arrive at 6 a.m. to carry on working on the house.

Christabel, interviewed in Paris where she was hiding from the possibility of prosecution, was asked if the WSPU minded being described as anarchists. 'We do not mind at all,' she replied, 'we are fighting a revolution.' She explained that Lloyd George was a primary target because, while often claiming to be in favour of women's suffrage, 'he was always betraying us'.

The perpetrators of the bombing were never caught, but, because of Emmeline's public confession, she was arrested for procuring and inciting women to commit offences contrary to the Malicious Injuries to Property Act. On 3 April she was sentenced to three years' penal servitude and immediately went on hunger strike.

There was no attempt to feed her forcibly and a new law was rapidly introduced to ensure she did not die in prison and become a martyr for the cause. The Prisoners Temporary Discharge for Ill Health Bill was rushed through to enable prisoners on hunger strike to be released when their health began to fail, give them time to recover and then return them to prison. It came to be known as the Cat and Mouse Act.

In August 1914, as the First World War began, the WSPU suspended its campaign. A letter to members said, 'Even the most vigorous militancy is rendered less effective by contrast with the infinitely greater violence done in the present war.' *The Suffragette*, the newspaper that had been edited by Christabel, was renamed *Britannia* with 'For King, For Country, For Freedom' as its slogan.

Emmeline campaigned for the widening of work available to women in support of the war effort and she, together with a number of other WSPU members, accepted the request of Lloyd George to organise a Women's Right to Serve demonstration to help overcome trade union opposition to the employment of female labourers. Lloyd George was the first senior politician to occupy the newly created post of Minister of Munitions, a job he held from 1915 to 1916. He was so successful at increasing the production of shells for the battlefield – work which included female labourers – that he boosted morale and raised his profile, contributing to his rise to Prime Minister in December 1916.

His elevation to the top job encouraged the suffragists to restore the campaign for women to have the right to vote in 1917. Asquith, the previous Prime Minister, had been implacably opposed to women's enfranchisement. Lloyd George, they thought, had dillied and dallied and made promises which had not been fulfilled, but they believed him, essentially, to have sympathy for the cause. The suffragists lobbied the coalition government like mad to ensure that women – or at least those over the age of thirty – would be included in the proposed new Representation of the People Bill.

The WSPU was renamed in 1917 as the Women's Party. *Britannia* became its official newspaper, edited by Christabel. On 6 February 1918 Royal Assent was given to the Act, which allowed women over the age of thirty the vote if they were house-holders, the wives of householders, occupiers of property with an annual rent of £5 or more, or graduates of British universities. Only 8.5 million women were included, but it was clear to all the suffrage campaigners that the first step had been taken and full citizenship for all women could not be far away.

Emmeline was keen that Christabel should become the first female Member of Parliament. Of her three daughters it was only Christabel who was in tune with their mother's politics. She fought the Smethwick constituency on the Women's Party ticket in the autumn general election and lost, but narrowly.

In 1924, after a hectic time during which Emmeline had lectured on social hygiene in Canada, where there were terrible worries about the number of men returning from the war with venereal infections, her health began to fail. She was sixty-six and had added to her responsibilities by taking in a small group of girls who had been orphaned during the war. It proved too much for her. Two of the girls were given up for adoption by well-off families, Christabel adopted one of the others, Betty, while another, Mary, stayed with Emmeline until 1928.

Emmeline returned to London in 1925 and was invited to stand as a Conservative candidate. She accepted the offer of the socialist working-class district of Whitechapel and St George's, knowing she couldn't win. When she was campaigning in the spring of 1928 she was shocked to learn from the *News of the World* that Sylvia had given birth to a son out of wedlock. She was heckled during her campaign about her immoral and wayward daughter, but dismissed the comments by saying she would not discuss private matters in public. She was never reconciled with Sylvia and saw her behaviour as an absolute disgrace. Adela had already gone to live in Australia. Only Christabel remained close to her mother.

In late May of 1928 Emmeline became very ill and was taken to a nursing home at 43 Wimpole Street where she died on 14 June from septicaemia contracted after a bout of flu. She was a month short of her seventieth birthday and only a couple of weeks away from seeing the full enfranchisement she had worked so hard to achieve. On 2 July 1928 the second Representation of the People Act gave voting rights to women over the age of twenty-one on equal terms with men.

Emmeline Pankhurst was buried in Brompton Cemetery in London and in March 1930 the Conservative Prime Minister, Stanley Baldwin, unveiled a bronze statue of her in Victoria Tower Gardens. It's a public park close to the River Thames and adjacent to the Victoria Tower on the south-western corner of the Palace of Westminster. There she is, to be remembered forever, close to the Houses of Parliament, whose closed doors she had made such efforts to open to women and win for us all the right to take our place as full citizens of Britain.

'I feel I must fight for *Der Wald* . . . because
I want women to turn their minds to big
and difficult jobs; not just go on hugging
the shore, afraid to put out to sea.'

Ethel Smyth

# 14

## Ethel Smyth

### 1858–1944

Even today it's difficult for a woman to be recognised as a composer of serious music. One of the most striking remarks I found among the paper archive that records every word said on *Woman's Hour* in its earliest days from 1946 came from Elisabeth Lutyens, who spoke about her ambition to become a great composer and her hope that she would also be able to become a wife and mother. It was, she thought, unlikely that both would be open to her as she would have to choose one or the other. She faced, she said, 'the tyranny of choice'. A choice that would not have to be faced by a man.

It was not a tyranny that troubled Dame Ethel Smyth, generally considered the most notable and successful of all the British women of the nineteenth and twentieth centuries who were recognised for their composition. She was open about her preference for passionate relationships with women, never married and never had a child.

She was born in London, the fourth of eight children in a military family. Her father, Major-General John Hall Smyth, and her mother, Emma, encouraged their children to enjoy sport and the outdoors. She lived at home with her parents in Sidcup in Kent and later in Frimley in Surrey and, I suppose, you could describe her as something of a tomboy. She played tennis, cricket and golf, which she continued to love into her old age. She was an enthusiastic hunter and was a pioneer of cycling – this at a time when it was considered an unsuitable mode of transport for a young woman. Smoking – also shocking in a young woman – was a habit she did not give up until 1899, when she was forty-one.

Ethel and her siblings were educated at home and there was no more musical education than would have been expected for a girl of her class. She learned to sing and play the piano, but when she was twelve a new governess came to teach her who had studied at the Leipzig conservatory. Ethel began to realise she had talent and ambition in the field of music. When she was fourteen she was sent to school in Putney for three years and, again, her musical education was pretty conventional and undemanding, but when she returned to Frimley a new tutor, Alexander Ewing, encouraged her to develop her musical abilities. She determined to travel to Leipzig to study composition.

As she reached her late teenage years her father expected her to follow the usual social conventions that would lead to a suitable marriage. There were endless rows about how improper it would be for an unmarried nineteen-year-old woman to travel alone to Germany with the intention of training for a career. Ethel was as determined to go as her father was determined she should not. She locked herself in her room when any social engagement loomed and refused to attend. General Smyth gave up the battle and agreed, finally, that she should go. She left for Leipzig in July 1877.

She stayed the course for less than a year, saying later that she had found both staff and students at the conservatory boring and unexciting. She had an alternative. She began to study privately with the composer Heinrich von Herzogenberg, who taught her harmony and counterpoint. He and his wife, Lisl, were respected in Germany's musical society and Brahms was one of their closest friends. She loved the social life to which the Herzogenbergs were able to introduce her and had no qualms about collecting a group of useful friends around her. The crème de la crème of Leipzig's musical élite would prove extremely beneficial to a young, ambitious would-be composer.

It was during this period that she had her first love affair. Heinrich and Lisl had no children to care for and invited Ethel to come and live with them in their home. She stayed there from 1878 to 1885 and she and Lisl became very close – more than merely good friends. Ethel saw no reason to be coy about her affairs. In her memoirs, *Impressions that Remained*, published in England in 1919, she wrote about her relationships, saying 'from the first my most ardent sentiments were bestowed on members of my own sex'.

There was one relationship with a man, which would eventually cause a great deal of heartache for Ethel and Lisl when the truth about what had been going on came out. Ethel lived with the Herzogenbergs for most of the year, but went home to England or travelled around Europe in the summer. In 1882 she met Lisl's sister Julia and her husband, Henry Brewster, in Florence. Henry was an American writer and philosopher who had been raised in France and it quickly became obvious that he fancied Ethel like mad. The following winter, in Italy, she stopped resisting his advances.

Even for free-thinking Ethel, it was obviously a step too far to be involved with the wife of one marriage and the husband of another. She tried to break with Brewster, but failed and, inevitably, as the two married couples had such a close family connection, the affair was discovered. Lisl found out what had been going on with her brother-in-law and in 1885 brought her relationship with Ethel to a dramatic close, weeping and crying out that she never wanted to see her again. The free accommodation in Leipzig was no longer available.

Rather conveniently, within a few years Lisl died. Her sister Julia died in 1895, and Ethel and Brewster were able openly to pursue the relationship they'd continued to carry on in secret. They lived in separate homes – he in Italy, she in England – and they neither married nor had children, but he was a steady companion throughout her life until he died in 1908. In her second volume of autobiography, *What Happened Next*, published in 1940, she wrote, 'Harry was never jealous of my women friends, in fact he held, as I do, that every new affection that comes into your life enriches older ties.'

Smyth's musical career had some success during her Leipzig years. She was strongly influenced by Brahms and she wrote lieder, piano music and a number of pieces for chamber ensembles. Most of them were performed for friends in private homes, but a violin sonata and a string quintet were performed in public at the Leipzig Gewandhaus.

When she returned to England in the late 1880s she had to build a reputation all over again and she managed to create quite a stir. At the Crystal Palace in 1890 her Serenade and Overture to *Antony and Cleopatra* were well received, as was her Mass, premiered in 1893 by the Royal Choral Society. This, she said, had been written during a resurgence of her Anglican faith after a religious crisis. The phase did not last. Composing the Mass, she wrote, had worked it out of her system. 'Orthodox belief fell away from me, never to return.'

Influence with the Royal Family had secured the performance of the Mass, as the Prince of Wales was patron of the Royal Choral Society. Friendships with a network of well-connected women also helped Ethel throughout her career. A neighbour in Farnborough where Ethel had set up home was the former Empress of France, Eugenie, the widow of Napoleon III, who lived in exile in England until her death. She helped Ethel fund publication of her works and made introductions to royalty and the aristocracy. Mary Ponsonby, one of Queen Victoria's women of the bedchamber, was another ardent patron. She and Ethel conducted an intimate and often stormy friendship for more than thirty years.

Ethel was encouraged, after the performance of the Mass, to develop her dramatic talent by the German composer Hermann Levi, who was a great supporter of her work. She embarked on her first opera, together with Brewster, who wrote the libretto. It was based on the play *Fantasio* by Alfred de Musset, and was accepted for performance at the court theatre in Weimar. The opera was well received there and again, in 1901, in Karlsruhe, but in *What Happened Next* she explained that, despite 'an almost perfect performance', she was not satisfied with the work as her music had 'too much passion and violence for a comic subject'.

Her second opera, also written in collaboration with Brewster, was *Der Wald*. It was a tragic love story and was said by critics to owe a debt to Wagner. When it was premiered in Berlin she had a terrible time: the audience hissed and the Berlin critics were unimpressed. There had been problems at the theatre and the opera was under-rehearsed when it came to its first performance, but she also claimed that she was a victim of sex discrimination and Anglophobia as a result of the Boer War.

*Der Wald* was better received in New York, Boston and Covent Garden and her name as a composer of opera was made, but she wrote to Brewster explaining what a struggle she'd been through. 'I feel I must fight for *Der Wald* . . . because I want women to turn their minds to big and difficult jobs; not just go on hugging the shore, afraid to put out to sea.'

Her greatest work is her third opera, *The Wreckers*. It's set on the coast of Cornwall in the eighteenth century and tells the tragic tale of lovers who try to stop the practice of wrecking, whereby locals would lure ships onto the rocks by lighting false beacons. The couple are caught and sentenced to death.

Again Brewster wrote the libretto, but, even though the story was an English one, it was written in French, perhaps a result of Smyth's increasing fascination with France and a group of eminent Parisian women, including the Princesse de Polignac, who was a noted patron of the arts, and a poet, Anna de Noailles.

The musical influences in this work are a mixture of styles ranging from what she learned in Germany to the contemporary style of France and English folk tunes.

*The Wreckers* was performed in Germany and in Prague, and was well received. Ethel always emphasised her successes in Europe as it seemed essential for an English composer to be valued abroad before he or she might be lauded in their home country. Covent Garden didn't accept the opera, saying it dared not take the financial risk of putting on a performance, but a wealthy American friend, Mary Dodge, offered to back a production at Her Majesty's Theatre. The young Thomas Beecham was hired to conduct and the piece was premiered in London on 22 June 1909. The following year it was staged at Covent Garden as part of the Beecham season.

It is hardly surprising, given her passionate support of the advancement of the independent woman, that Ethel became an enthusiastic member of the Women's Social and Political Union and developed a close association with Emmeline Pankhurst. For two years, from 1911, she put her career aside to work for the WSPU and raised funds by putting on concerts. She also drew on the sporting experiences she'd had as a child.

Ethel had been a mean bowler in the games of cricket she'd played with her brothers and their friends. A woman, Christina Willes, had invented overarm bowling in the early nineteenth century. She had played with her brother, John, a member of the Kent and England teams, and Christina bowled overarm so that the ball wouldn't get caught in her skirts. We can assume Ethel would have known the technique. It came in handy when Emmeline Pankhurst announced that smashing windows with stones would become a policy of the suffragettes and needed someone to teach her and her fellow revolutionaries how to throw with accuracy. Ethel was a willing teacher and practitioner and served a short time in prison for her crime.

It was as a suffragette that Ethel wrote the music for which she is probably best known. 'The March of the Women' was dedicated to the WSPU and begins:

> Shout, shout, up with your song,
> Cry with the wind for the dawn is breaking;
> March, march, swing you along,
> Wide blows our banner, and hope is waking.
> Song with its story, dreams with their glory,
> Lo! they call, and glad is their word!
> Loud and louder it swells,
> Thunder of freedom, the voice of the Lord!

The fourth verse ends with 'Firm in reliance, laugh in defiance / (Laugh in hope, for sure is the end) / March, march – many as one, / Shoulder to shoulder and friend to friend.' During her stay in Holloway Prison, serving her time for her stone-throwing activities, Thomas Beecham went to visit her and found, on entering the main courtyard, a crowd of suffragettes 'marching around it and singing lustily their war chant while the composer, beaming approbation from an overlooking window, beat time in almost Bacchic frenzy with a toothbrush'.

There was one more opera, composed just before the start of the First World War, called *The Boatswain's Mate*. Ethel wrote the libretto herself and the story is a battle of the sexes between the female owner of a pub, Mrs Waters, and a retired boatswain, Harry Benn, whose offers of marriage she has rejected. It was not performed in Germany, for obvious reasons, but was staged in London in 1916, revived after the war, and included in the repertory of the Old Vic in the 1920s. The critics never raved about it, but her suffragette friends loved it and it's now considered her most feminist and most popular work.

During the war Smyth worked in Paris as a radiographer. She

also began to suffer problems with her hearing, which would worsen as she got older. She began to write her memoirs, which turned out to be a great success and brought her a useful amount of money when her hearing began to affect her ability to compose. Her books were well liked, perhaps because their content was rather racy. I can find no evidence of any shocked critique of her openness about her lesbian affairs.

Between 1921 and 1940 Ethel wrote a number of volumes of memoir, numerous opinionated articles and made money from her travel writing, including descriptions of a journey on a camel in the Egyptian desert and hikes in the wilder parts of Greece. The writing brought new audiences to her music, inspired new performances of the work and introduced her as a conductor in the concert hall and theatre.

As she said in one of her articles, Ethel was grateful that she had had 'a small independent income which rendered possible a continuous struggle for musical existence such as no woman obliged to earn her livelihood in music could have carried on'.

There were a few more musical works in the 1920s and '30s and numerous performances of her earlier work, but, as she grew older, Ethel became increasingly bitter that her achievements as a composer had not been recognised as they should have been. She was, though, celebrated with a festival of her music on her seventy-fifth birthday, which was also broadcast on the BBC.

Her final years were spent in her cottage in Woking, still dressed in her tweed suits and battered hats and doting on a series of large dogs, beginning with Marco and ending with a number of Old English sheepdogs, all of whom she called Pan. She was made a Dame in 1922 for her contribution to music, but still felt she lacked recognition. An Austrian critic, Richard Specht, wrote of her in 1911:

This thin resolute woman, touched by no sense of the 'shocking', who laughs at all the follies of the world . . . one is aware that she has lived alone for many years with her big dog . . . in a lonely cottage and thus has become a piece of English nature herself.

Smyth died in her cottage in Woking from pneumonia at the age of eighty-six. She would, I'm sure, be delighted to know that the musical and feminist academic establishments have, in recent years, begun to re-evaluate her musical achievements and concluded that she was indeed a great composer who stood in a line that includes Clara Schumann, Fanny Mendelssohn, Amy Beach and Elizabeth Maconchy.

Critics have often been dismissive of the work of these women, saying there are no 'great' female composers because genius is rare, whether the practitioner is male or female, and there have been too few female composers for a genius to emerge. There may be something in that theory as Mozart, Bach and Haydn are rarities among the hundreds of men who made it into the musical canon. I've listened to some of Smyth's work and I wouldn't class her as a genius, but to deny she's great seems to me a simple case of misogynist prejudice.

'I do wish your lot had the decency to shoot me.'

Constance Markievicz

# 15

## Constance Markievicz

### 1868–1927

It's often assumed that Nancy Astor was the first woman elected to the British Parliament in 1919. She was indeed the first female MP to occupy her seat in the House of Commons, as we'll see in a later chapter, but the first to be elected was Constance Markievicz, who won her seat in the 1918 general election, but, as a member of Sinn Féin, she obeyed the Irish Republican Party's policy of abstention and never attended.

Constance Georgina Gore-Booth was one of four children born to Sir Henry Gore-Booth of Lissadell in County Sligo and his wife, Georgina Mary. The Gore-Booths were a wealthy English family who had owned land in Sligo since the seventeenth century. They were not, though, the kind of absentee landlords who had so abandoned their Irish peasant workers during the Famine of the mid-nineteenth century. Constance was raised by parents who taught her to care for and respect those less fortunate than themselves.

And the Gore-Booth girls were indeed fortunate. They were cultured, sporty and beautiful, and she and her sister, Eva, had a very close relationship. They inspired W. B. Yeats who, in 1927, wrote 'In Memory of Eva Gore-Booth and Con Markiewicz', describing the sisters as 'Two girls in silk kimonos, both / Beautiful, one a gazelle.'

Like their contemporaries in the late nineteenth century, the girls were educated at home and taught music, poetry and art. In 1887 they were taken by their governess on a typically aristocratic grand tour of Europe and, upon their return, were expected to fulfil their duties as good, high-class girls. They would be presented at court, make good marriages and spend the rest of their lives as wives, mothers and society hostesses.

Constance was presented to Queen Victoria at Buckingham Palace in 1887, but neither she nor her sister did what was expected of a debutante. Constance had plenty of offers of a 'suitable' marriage, but turned down all her suitors. Like Ethel Smyth, she had to fight her family to achieve what she wanted. She was determined, she told her father, to study art and in 1893 he relented and she was enrolled in the Slade School of Fine Art in London.

The women's suffrage movement was beginning to bubble – only ten years later the Women's Social and Political Union would be founded – and Constance was drawn to the arguments of the suffragists. By 1896 she was presiding over a meeting of the Sligo Women's Suffrage Society.

In 1898 she went to Paris to carry on studying art and it was there she met Count Casimir Dunin-Markievicz, a wealthy Polish national whose family owned land in Ukraine. They married in 1900, had their only child, a daughter, Maeve, in 1901 and then returned to Dublin as a family in 1902. The two of them became involved in Dublin's cultural and political life. Casimir and Constance produced and acted in plays at the Abbey Theatre, helped found the United Arts Club and exhibited their own artistic work.

Constance's political life became increasingly radical after she rented a cottage in the countryside outside Dublin in 1906. A set of leaflets had been left behind by a previous tenant. The title of the series of pamphlets was 'The Peasant and Sinn Féin' and the text advocated independence from British rule. She was soon persuaded of the cause.

Constance was introduced in 1908 to Helena Molony and an organisation called Inghinidhe na hÉireann (Daughters of Ireland). Molony had been spurred into feminist and republican activity by Maud Gonne, the English-born revolutionary, suffragette, actor and inspiring speaker, perhaps best remembered for her turbulent relationship with Yeats.

The group had grown from a campaign to organise a 'patriotic children's treat' for children who boycotted Queen Victoria's visit to Ireland in 1900. It warned girls against consorting with British soldiers, pressed local shops into stocking Irish rather than British goods and set out to persuade boys that the British Army was not a suitable career. Constance was a founder of the monthly newspaper published by the group, *Bean na hÉireann* (*Women of Ireland*), said to be committed to 'militancy, separatism and feminism'. She wrote articles about gardening for the publication. She also joined Sinn Féin.

In 1909 Constance played an important role in the formation of the Irish Boy Scouts Movement. Its stated aim was to train boys in drill and the firing of rifles, teach them to engage with the Irish language and culture and prepare themselves to help in the establishment of an independent and united Ireland. By 1911 she was a member of the executive of Sinn Féin and was arrested while protesting against the visit of King George V to Dublin.

Constance's politics began to move further to the left and she worked closely with James Connolly in the growing trade union movement. In 1911 she spoke at the meeting to establish the Irish Women Workers' Union and her house in Rathmines, a suburb to the south of Dublin, became a hotbed of nationalist and trade union activity. During the 1913 Lockout, where some twenty thousand workers had entered into dispute with around three hundred employers, she organised a soup kitchen in Liberty Hall and joined the newly founded Irish Citizen Army, a voluntary group of trade union members trained to protect the demonstrators.

By 1914 Constance realised revolution was brewing and she was instrumental in the merging of the two main women's organisations, Cumann na mBan and Inghinidhe na hÉireann, into one. Cumann na mBan, the Irishwomen's Council, began to define itself as an Irish women's paramilitary organisation, which in 1916 became an auxiliary of the Irish Volunteers, the group led by Éamon de Valera that would become the Irish Republican Army (IRA).

At the outbreak of the Great War she and her husband separated. He went to the Balkans to work as a war reporter and their daughter went to Sligo to be cared for by her grandparents, leaving Constance free to pursue her political aims. She had no difficulties in espousing military action to break Ireland's link with Britain, and by 1916 she was ready to be an active participant in the Easter Rising.

On Easter Monday, 24 April 1916, Constance loaded up Dr Kathleen Lynn's car with first aid kits and, as she described it, 'drove off through quiet dusty streets and across the river, reaching City Hall'. She reported to Michael Mallin who was second in command of the Irish Citizen Army and in charge of the St Stephen's Green Garrison. The occupation of St Stephen's Green, the public park at the centre of Dublin, was already well under way. She remained there for a week, effectively becoming Mallin's deputy. She organised the defence of the park and is reputed to have shot a policeman. By early Tuesday the situation of the rebels in St Stephen's Green was deteriorating. The British had taken control of the buildings surrounding the park, including the Shelbourne Hotel.

The garrison came under increasing fire, so they retreated to the Royal College of Surgeons where they would spend the rest of the week. On the Sunday morning, Elizabeth O'Farrell, a nurse and prominent member of the Irishwomen's Council, led the surrender. She walked from Grafton Street towards the college, carrying a white flag. She handed the surrender note to Markievicz who read it and handed it in turn to Mallin. O'Farrell took the note to the other volunteer outposts in the city, Mallin ordered the white flag to be flown from the college and Captain Henry de Courcy-Wheeler – a distant relative of the Gore-Booths – arrived to accept the surrender. He met Mallin and Markievicz at the college door. She kissed her pistol and handed it to the Captain before being marched to Richmond Barracks along with her fellow insurgents.

Markievicz was the only woman tried in a court martial after the Easter Rising. She defended herself in court by saying, 'I went out for Ireland's freedom and it doesn't matter what happens to me. I did what I thought was right and I stand by it.' She was sentenced to death, but it was decided that, because of her gender, her sentence would be commuted to life imprisonment. It's said the British government had been criticised so often for the cruel treatment of suffragettes during the force-feeding period that they were afraid to execute a prominent woman.

No such sentiment applied to the male rebel leaders. Her commander during the rising, Michael Mallin, was executed by firing squad on 8 May 1916. He was forty-one and left a family including his mother, three siblings, a pregnant wife and four children. Constance heard the firing squads do their work from her cell and is reported to have said, 'I do wish your lot had the decency to shoot me.'

She was transferred from Kilmainham Gaol to Mountjoy and then to Aylesbury Prison in England. She took instruction in Catholicism while in prison and was released under the general amnesty in June 1917, having served fourteen months of her life sentence.

Markievicz soon resumed her political activities. She was elected again to the executive of Sinn Féin and became president of Cumann na mBan. In 1918 she was arrested again for alleged involvement in the 'German plot'. The Dublin Castle administration in Ireland claimed a conspiracy had been hatched between the Sinn Féin movement and the German Empire to start an armed insurrection in Ireland during the Great War.

There was no hard evidence that such a plot existed; indeed it's now generally regarded as a 'black propaganda' project to discredit Sinn Féin. The arrests proved counter-productive for the British. The more accommodating members of the Sinn Féin leadership were caught and imprisoned, while those more committed to physical force had been forewarned and escaped. The whole incident enabled Michael Collins to consolidate his control of Sinn Féin and put the IRA on a more focused military footing to continue the guerrilla war of Irish independence, which went on from January 1919 to July 1921.

It was during her second period of residing at His Majesty's Pleasure that Constance stood for election as a Sinn Féin candidate for Dublin's St Patrick's division in the 1918 general election. She won, becoming the first woman elected to the British Parliament, but never took her seat. She was released from prison in March 1919 and was appointed Minister of Labour in the first Irish Parliament – the Dáil Éireann, which declared itself independent from Britain. There would not be another woman minister in the Irish Parliament until Máire Geoghegan-Quinn was appointed to the Cabinet by Charles Haughey in 1979.

Her fighting spirit had not been quelled by the experiences following 1916. She continued her opposition to British rule in Ireland and was arrested in 1919 for making a seditious speech and sentenced to four months' hard labour. In September 1920 she was arrested again and, this time, sentenced to two years' hard labour. She was released in July 1921 during the truce when de Valera and Lloyd George negotiated the Anglo-Irish Treaty.

Constance was vehemently opposed to the Treaty and gave a storming performance in the Dáil, condemning it and advocating an Irish Workers' Republic. She took the side of the Anti-Treaty IRA during the Civil War, which lasted from June 1922 to May

1923. It ended with victory for those in favour of the Treaty and the foundation of the Irish Free State.

Constance was re-elected to the Dáil in 1923, but refused to take the Oath of Allegiance to the British crown, so, again, didn't take her seat in Parliament. Later that year she was arrested for the fourth time because she'd been trying to collect signatures for a petition demanding the release of republican prisoners. In jail she went on hunger strike until she and her fellow prisoners were released.

In 1926 de Valera formed Fianna Fáil, a centre-right republican party which split from Sinn Féin on the issue of abstentionism – the very reason Constance, as a Sinn Féin member, had refused her seats in the British Parliament and the Dáil. She broke her ties with Sinn Féin and Cumann na mBan and joined Fianna Fáil. It's unclear why her militancy was tempered, but in 1927 during the general election she campaigned and was elected to the Dáil as a Fianna Fáil candidate.

Her long years of fighting, terms in prison and hunger strikes had begun to take their toll on her health. The previous year, during a coal strike, she had spent her time trudging around Dublin bringing food and fuel to the city's poor. Her sister Eva had died that year and Constance was beset by grief, and she quickly became extremely ill after the death of her closest companion. In 1927 she was admitted to Sir Patrick Dun's hospital, insisting on being cared for in the public ward as a pauper. She was fifty-nine when she died in July.

She lay in state in the Pillar Room of the Rotunda Rink in Dublin where the Irish Volunteers had been launched. It was a temporary building in the Rotunda Gardens that could hold four thousand people, and many thousands went there to pay their respects to 'their countess'. Her funeral oration was delivered by Éamon de Valera and she was buried at Glasnevin Cemetery, Dublin.

The great playwright Séan O'Casey, who lived through and documented the war of independence in plays such as *The Shadow of a Gunman, The Plough and the Stars* and *Juno and the Paycock*, wrote of Constance Markievicz, 'One thing she had in abundance was physical courage: with that she was clothed as with a garment.'

It's perhaps surprising that a woman who had no love for Britain and the British should find her place in this history. She's here, not only because she was the first to be elected to the British Parliament, but because, like Boadicea, she gives the lie to the old idea that women are not capable of bearing arms and fighting for their beliefs and their countries. Her bravery and passion for the politics of an independent Ireland cannot be denied.

'Fifty years after my death I shall be
remembered as Gwen John's brother.'

Gwen John's brother

# 16

## Gwen John

### 1876–1939

Just as Ethel Smyth found female composers lacked recognition and were generally undervalued, so too did artists such as Gwen John find that their gender held them back. It's now pretty much accepted (not only by me, but by a significant portion of the art establishment) that Gwen was a better painter and a more affecting artist than her younger brother, Augustus, but she spent her lifetime in his shadow.

He, though, recognised her talent, saying that 'her pictures are almost painfully charged with feeling, whilst my own are almost painfully empty of it'. He also wrote of his awareness that she was always known as Augustus John's sister, but predicted that 'fifty years after my death I shall be remembered as Gwen John's brother'.

Gwen spent her early childhood in Haverfordwest, in Pembrokeshire, Wales, with her three siblings and her parents. Her father, Edwin, was a solicitor and her mother, Augusta, an amateur artist. Augusta died when Gwen was only eight and the family moved to Tenby where the children were first educated at home by a governess. All the John children were delighted to leave home as soon as possible. Edwin was far from a cheery character and ruled his household with strict discipline, so their home was a depressing place to be. After his wife's death he neglected the children and Augustus was aware of how unhappy his mother had been in her marriage: 'My mother would no doubt have been helpful, but she died when I was a small child, after, I fear, a very tearful existence.'

Gwen spent some time at a school in Tenby, then in an educational establishment in London run by a Miss Philpott. She then, at the age of nineteen, won a place at the Slade School of Fine Art, the most sought-after and most progressive art college in Britain. It was the only such school that allowed female students, but men and women didn't mix in classes, corridors or in the grounds. Just as a girl in an anatomy theatre was found unacceptable in Elizabeth Garrett Anderson's education, there was no place for Gwen in a life drawing class. She stuck it out for three years and was a great success, winning a certificate for figure drawing and the Melville Nettleship prize for figure composition.

But even at college she was overshadowed by Augustus. He was younger, but he had preceded her to the art school and, while he had an easy circle of friends and, throughout his life, lovers – he once said he always patted the heads of children he saw in Chelsea in case they were his – she was shy and quiet. Nor did she dress or behave in the racy, bohemian manner favoured by Augustus and his chums. Her self-portraits show a rather thin, pinched face, a severe hairstyle, parted down the middle and tied back, and a modest frock buttoned up to the neck.

Gwen and her brother shared a flat during their student years to save money and no doubt to free Augustus from any responsibility for the housework. They lived sparsely on a diet of nuts and fruit, and while Augustus was always full of praise for the quality of her work, he worried that she neglected her health and asked her to 'take a more athletic attitude to life'. She took no notice of his advice. She is often described as meek and self-effacing, slight and pale with solemn, watchful dark eyes. Her self-portraits, though, now on show at Tate Britain and the National Portrait Gallery, do suggest a rather determined personality.

Gwen went to Paris when she had completed her studies at the Slade and spent several months at the Académie Carmen where she was taught by James McNeill Whistler, who admired her 'fine sense of tone'. His influence on the style of her work seems clear to me when looking at his most famous painting, *Arrangement in Grey and Black No. 1*, popularly known as 'Whistler's Mother'.

After Paris, Gwen returned to London in January 1899 and for four years lived what she described as a 'subterranean' exist-ence in a series of gloomy rooms in Bloomsbury and Bayswater, even at one point living as a squatter in a derelict building. It was a miserable period. She had a disastrous love affair with a fellow painter, Ambrose McEvoy, and wrote in a letter to a friend in Aberystwyth, 'As to being happy . . . when a picture is done, whatever it is, it might as well not be as far as the artist is concerned – and in all the time he has taken to do it, it has only given him a few seconds' pleasure . . . People are like shadows to me and I am like a shadow.'

As the century turned from the nineteenth to the twentieth she exhibited for the first time in the spring of 1900 at the New English Art Club and continued to show there twice a year until 1903, although she was never keen on exhibitions apart, of course, for the money they generated. In March of that year Gwen and her brother had a joint exhibition and her reputation for working extremely slowly was borne out. He produced forty-five works for display. She came up with only three. 'I paint a good deal,' she once said, 'but I don't often get a picture done. That requires, for me, a very long time of a quiet mind, and never to think of exhibitions.'

Gwen was adventurous enough to want to see more of the world, although she never got very far. In the autumn of 1903 she and a friend, Dorelia McNeill, who would later become Augustus's second wife, decided they would go travelling together and make their living from their work as they went around. They took their art equipment, landed in Bordeaux and set off on a walking tour with the intention of reaching Rome. They slept in fields and made enough money for food by selling portrait sketches. They got as far as Toulouse and then decided to go to Paris in 1904.

Gwen lived a classically bohemian existence in a series of modest residences in Montparnasse, several of them appearing in her paintings, perhaps most famously *A Corner of the Artist's Room in Paris*, which is now in Sheffield's Graves Gallery. She decided to cut herself off from her family and from England, declaring it 'quite a foreign country', and she earned her living as an artist's model. She worked mostly for women painters, but also for a small number of men, including the most famous artist of the time, the sculptor Auguste Rodin.

She was the archetypal model who became the artist's lover and, although he was thirty-six years her senior, their affair continued for ten years. Gwen clung to Rodin even after he had become bored with her devotion. There are thousands of letters that she wrote to him, pouring out her passion long after she had become a millstone around his neck. 'Love is my illness,' she wrote, 'and there is no cure until you come.' She had a habit throughout her life of attaching herself to people who would have preferred an arm's-length relationship, and Rodin was no exception. He became so frustrated by her dogged insistence that they should remain lovers, he ordered his secretary, and bribed the concierge in his building, to deny her entry and keep her away. The affair finally came to an end in 1914, three years before his death.

Her obsession with Rodin took up all her energy during those ten years from 1904 to 1914 and she wrote, again to a friend, 'Everything interests me more than painting. I am quite frightened by my coldness towards painting which gets worse and worse.' She did, though, manage some of her best work during this period, perhaps a dozen paintings, including the stunning *Girl*

*Reading at a Window*, which is now in the Museum of Modern Art in New York.

During her years in Paris she got to know all the leading artists of the time, including Matisse and Picasso, but Gwen was never influenced by the new movements in modern art. She worked by herself and stuck to her own style. She lived in France for the rest of her life, but was never drawn into the avant-garde movements in art, theatre and music that were such a feature of the French capital in the early twentieth century. Indeed, one art critic said her work always displayed a British sensibility.

She wrote in a letter in 1916, 'I think a picture ought to be done in one sitting or at the most two. For that one must paint a lot of canvases probably and waste them.' The majority of her work is portraits, but there are a few still life studies, interiors and landscapes. On subject matter she wrote, 'a cat or a man, it's her same thing . . . it's an affair of volumes . . . the object is of no importance.' Nevertheless, the most common subject matter for her paintings is young women, generally alone, sitting down with their hands in their laps.

One of her models, Jeanne Foster, said of her, 'She takes down my hair and does it like her own . . . she has made me sit as she does, and I feel the absorption of her personality as I sit.' As her brother said, 'all her pictures are almost painfully charged with feeling', and it seems from what Foster says that the painful feelings were her own. Only 158 of her oil paintings are known to have survived.

In the twilight of Gwen's love affair with Rodin she began to focus more on her own painting: the next decade would prove highly fruitful. Augustus introduced her paintings to an American lawyer and collector, John Quinn. From 1911 he provided her with patronage and bought any picture she offered, acquiring around a dozen paintings and lots of drawings. The two didn't meet until

1921, but his admiration for her work gave her emotional support and introductions to a wide circle of friends. Her professional relationship and friendship with Quinn lasted until he died in 1924 and coincides with the most productive time of her life.

In 1911 Gwen found rooms in the Paris suburb of Meudon where Rodin lived. She took instruction in Catholicism and around 1913 was received into the Roman Catholic Church. Her notebooks from the period include meditations and prayers and hint at her desire to 'become God's little artist' and to 'become a saint'. In 1912 she wrote, 'As to whether I have anything worth expressing . . . I may never have anything to express, except this desire for a more interior life.'

As a result of her connection with the Church she was invited by the nuns of the locality to paint a series of portraits of the founder of the Sœurs de la Charité Dominicaines, Mère Marie Poussepin. Six are known to have survived. She also painted scores of watercolours of church interiors populated by the nuns and the little orphan girls who were in their care, and all of them are typically painted from behind. She said, 'I am in love with the atmosphere of Meudon Church and the people who go to church there have a charm for me (especially when I don't speak to them).' There's that shy, uncommunicative woman again.

Gwen spent the years of the First World War in Paris, making occasional trips to the seaside in Brittany where she made deeply moving pictures of the local children. The war meant she was unable to exhibit in London, but two exhibitions were mounted in New York.

Her confidence in her ability as an artist seemed to blossom in the early 1920s, perhaps as a result of the continued support and admiration of John Quinn. She exhibited in the Paris salons and in the Sculptors Gallery in New York in 1922 thanks to Quinn. She never went to America, but she wrote to him regularly and told him how content she was in her milieu. 'I am quite in my work now and think of nothing else. I paint until it is dark . . . and then I have supper and then I read about an hour and think of my painting . . . I like this life very much.' In another letter, she showed her growing self-confidence: 'I was very pleased and proud of my "Mère Poussepin". I thought it the best picture there, but I liked the Seurat landscape.' Of an exhibition of Cézanne's watercolours she wrote, 'These are very good, but I prefer my own.'

This happy and confident period seems to have come to an end in 1924 when John Quinn died. The financial security he had given her with a regular stipend and sales of her work was over. She painted less, and without the encouragement of Quinn was reluctant to exhibit. In 1926, though, a major exhibition was held at the New Chenil Galleries in London and there was a great deal of attention, generated, one suspects, by her brother who was at the top of his artistic game in London and still living a high old social life.

By 1930 Gwen's work was becoming familiar in great public collections, including the Tate, the Manchester City Gallery and others in Dublin, Buffalo and Chicago. Personally she became increasingly solitary, keeping up sporadically with some old friends and forming one last obsessive attachment. Her love object this time was Véra Oumançoff, the sister-in-law of a neighbour in Meudon. It was a strictly unrequited love affair and was ended around 1930 by Véra who couldn't stand Gwen's constant demands for attention.

There is no evidence that Gwen did any more work at all after 1933. She bought a derelict shack in Meudon with a patch of ground and lived there with her cats, often sleeping in the garden. She became increasingly and deliberately withdrawn, writing that her weaknesses were:

1. Sitting before people listening to them in an idiotic way.
2. Undergoing their influence – being what they expect – demande. 3. By fear flattering them. 4. Being too much

touched – valuing too much their signs of friendship, or rather responding too thoughtlessly. 5. Thinking too often of people.

She became a complete recluse, making occasional visits to Brittany, and it was on one of those trips that the woman who had so deliberately neglected her health and well-being fell ill and died in September 1939 in the Hospice de Dieppe. The death certificate does not specify a cause.

Gwen John was a wonderful painter who, like so many young women, then and now, found her ambition would always be considered secondary to that of a brother. Augustus was sent without question to art school in Tenby and then to the Slade, long before Gwen managed to get herself to London. But she was brave and determined enough to defy the expectations placed on a young woman of her time and did her own thing. As she said herself, 'I think if we are to do beautiful pictures, we ought to be free from family conventions and ties . . . I think the family has had its day. We don't go to Heaven in families now – but one by one.'

Her work is, as so many have said, quiet, private and reticent, but she was confident of her own genius. She described it with her usual self-deprecation: 'As to me, I cannot imagine why my vision will have some value in the world – and yet I know it will.' As indeed it does. We should, at last, be describing Augustus as 'Gwen John's brother'. She deserves it.

'He told me they hoped to freeze me out. It
felt, he said, like a woman had entered his
bathroom and he had nothing to protect
himself apart from his sponge. I told him he
was not handsome enough to have such fears!'

Nancy Astor on Churchill

# 17

# Nancy Astor

## 1879–1964

Ifirst encountered the wit and wisdom of Nancy Astor and the controversies and inconsistencies that often surrounded her during her political life when, in 2000, *Woman's Hour* broadcast an interview from the archive that she had given in 1956. The reason for the repeat was the eightieth anniversary of her maiden speech in the House of Commons. She was the first woman to take her seat in the British Parliament when she won the by-election in Plymouth Sutton in 1919.

Her husband, the millionaire Waldorf Astor, was American-born, but naturalised British. He had held the Plymouth seat, but when his father, Viscount Astor, died, Waldorf inherited his peerage, was forced to resign his seat and joined the House of Lords. Nancy agreed to stand in his place.

Nancy was also American, born as Nancy Witcher Langhorne. She was the eighth of eleven children of a Virginian railway businessman, Chiswell Langhorne, and his wife, Nancy. The family had not been wealthy when Nancy was born as her father's business, which is thought to have depended on slave labour, had folded as a result of the American Civil War. He worked hard to rebuild their resources, and by the time Nancy was thirteen they were a rich family again with a substantial estate in Albemarle County, Virginia.

Nancy and her sister Irene were sent to a finishing school in New York. It's curious that her expensive and high-quality education did nothing to temper her Virginian accent. In the 1956 interview, after years of living in England and mixing with the social crème de la crème, 'going to' still becomes 'gonna', 'them' is ''em' and she seems incapable of placing an 'ing' at the end of a word that requires it. Thus 'flirting' is 'flirtin'' and 'going' is 'goin''.

In New York she met her first husband, a wealthy socialite called Robert Gould Shaw, and they were married when Nancy was only eighteen. It was a disastrously unhappy marriage. They had one son, Robert Gould Shaw III, but her husband, according to their friends, was an alcoholic and an abuser. He was accused of raping and beating his wife.

They stayed together for four years. Nancy left him numerous times, the first time on their honeymoon, but kept going back. She left for good in 1901 and they were finally divorced in 1903. Her divorce coincided with the death of her mother and she went home to Virginia with the intention of running the estate. She did not prove a success at this and her father encouraged her to travel. She fell in love with England and decided to move to London permanently with her sister Phyllis in 1905.

It was not uncommon at the time for impoverished English aristocrats to marry wealthy Americans for their money. Unsurprisingly, Nancy was asked by an English woman at a social event, 'Have you come to get our husbands?' Nancy's response was, 'If you knew the trouble I had getting rid of mine . . . you'd know I don't want yours.' It's the first recorded example of the cutting wit for which she became famous and it seems to have gone down extremely well with the perhaps more reserved London socialites. She was beautiful, charming and funny – she was a hit.

Her marriage to Waldorf Astor took place in 1906 and lasted until his death in 1952. He had moved to England with his family at the age of twelve and had been raised as an English aristocrat. They were extremely well matched, even sharing the same birthday, 19 May 1879. The house they moved into after the wedding is now considered one of the most beautiful in England. Cliveden is an Italianate mansion and estate, which was a wedding gift from Waldorf's father. They also had a grand London house at 4 St James's Square in Westminster. Cliveden is huge and sits on the banks of the River Thames in Buckinghamshire. Its grounds are stunning and it was only in the twilight of Nancy's life, in 1963, that it became notorious.

It was where a number of incidents in the Profumo affair occurred. Christine Keeler and Mandy Rice Davies were invited to Cliveden as company for the powerful and wealthy men who met there. Keeler had an affair with John Profumo who was then Secretary of State for War. She was also allegedly involved in a dalliance with Yevgeny Ivanov, the Soviet naval attaché, and when the details came out in the press there were serious questions about whether national security had been breached as a result of pillow talk from Profumo to Keeler and thus on to Ivanov. The scandal brought down the Macmillan government and made Cliveden famous for all the wrong reasons. It has now restored its reputation, in a way. It's owned by the National Trust and is leased as a five-star hotel.

Nancy's son William, the third Viscount Astor, was accused of having an affair with Mandy Rice Davies. When she was told in court that he had denied the accusation Mandy gave her famous response, 'Well, he would, wouldn't he?' In Peter Stanford's book about the affair, Bronwen Astor, William's wife, lays the blame for her husband's 'little boy lost' persona on his domineering, possessive and formidable mother, who spoiled and indulged him at every turn. I guess it's always the mother who gets the blame.

In her interview with *Woman's Hour* Nancy was asked about her wealth and whether there was a degree of shame or criticism attached to being fabulously rich as a politician who concerned herself with the poor, particularly poverty-stricken children. Her answer was unequivocal:

> I adore bein' rich. During an election campaign someone yelled out one night, 'Mr Astor's a millionaire, ain't he!' Mr Astor was embarrassed, but I replied, 'I hope to God he is. It's one of the reasons I married him. Now come out an' show your face.' It seems to me most extraordinary that anyone should be ashamed of it.

> One rich woman went to the East End and put on her worst clothes. When I went to the East End I would have considered it rude not to wear my good clothes. People know you've got them. I think what people hate is pretence. Nobody is more proud of the progress in this country than I am and my contribution to it. What a joy it is not to see ragged children and children with their feet out.

Her constituents in Plymouth were, on the whole, remarkably tolerant about her wealth, knowing perhaps that her husband's family were well-respected philanthropists in the area. In her papers there are numerous letters from women detailing their hardships in the 1930s and evidence that Nancy sent them money. Not all her riches were given to good causes, though. There are in the same papers from the same period phenomenal bills from her jewellers and couturiers in London and Paris, and details of huge amounts of money spent on lavish entertaining in both London and at Cliveden.

By the time Nancy decided she would stand for Parliament in the by-election after her husband transferred from the Commons to the Lords, she and Waldorf had five children plus the son from her first marriage. She was asked, inevitably, during the campaign whether she should not be at home looking after her children. 'I feel someone ought to be looking after the unfortunate children,' she replied. 'My children are among the fortunate ones.'

Nancy campaigned enthusiastically and silenced her hecklers with rapid repartee. One who shouted out during one of her speeches, 'Call yourself a lady?' received the response, 'Certainly not!' She became the Conservative MP for Plymouth Sutton with a majority of 5,203 votes. In her election address she talked about how she had 'no personal ambition to go to Parliament' but had been encouraged by others. 'I intend,' she said, 'to work for the Peace, Progress and Prosperity of the country. I shall, at the same time, have due regard to National Efficiency and Economy which women above all understand.'

She took her seat in the House on 1 December 1919, led in between Arthur Balfour and Lloyd George. She received hundreds of letters of congratulation, but none from the suffragist movement. Constance Markievicz described her as 'of the upper classes and out of touch'. Christabel Pankhurst and a number of other women from the movement had stood in 1918 and none had been successful. There was a lot of anger that the first woman to make it was an extremely wealthy American with no political background at all. She was asked on *Woman's Hour* how it had felt to be that first woman, going there all alone.

Of course the suffragettes were disappointed. They didn't know me and had hoped for one of their own. Nobody was more distressed than I to be the first woman in the House. I'm a proud Virginian and would not have wanted an Englishwoman to be the first in my legislature. I apologised to Mrs Fawcett and so on. But the loyalty of the women surpassed all expectations.

How did I feel that first day? Well, I didn't mind the election at all. I liked that, but to walk up to the House between Arthur Balfour and Lloyd George, both of whom said they believed in women, but would rather have had a rattlesnake than me at that time. It was alarmin'. Sometimes I would sit for five hours in my seat not darin' to get down.

What kept me goin'? I was an ardent feminist. I always knew women have more moral strength. I said once in the House to the men we've got moral strength, you've got immoral strength. It was a bit rude, but I was often quite rude.

The suffragists and suffragettes soon came to accept Nancy Astor and recognise her value to the cause. There were frequent parties in St James's Square to which they were invited and Nancy was only too well aware of the usefulness of her phenomenal connections.

It's a jolly good thing I was the first. I knew everyone and could make introductions and advance things. I cared about social reform and knew the editors of the press as personal friends to get the ideas out. I could afford good secretaries. So much support to keep me up.

She was extremely isolated, never going to the bars and smoking rooms and wearing a simple uniform of jacket, skirt and white shirt. She explained her way of dressing was studied to give her credibility, and compared herself with some of the women who came in later.

One had a new dress every day, dressed more for Ascot than the House of Commons. And she flirted. Men don't like flirtin' in public. If I had been a sexy woman I wouldn't have lasted a week. Another woman was bustivi-ferous and the men said that at last they had a mother. I told 'em I had six children and she hadn't. You know they judge mothers by their figures sometimes and it's a mistake. They shouldn't.

Her maiden speech in February 1920 was on what she called 'that vexed question, Drink.' When she had first gone to Plymouth she could count ten public houses in one street. She also had a history of living with a violent drunk and it was not uncommon for temperance to be high on the female agenda, as it was well known that alcohol was at the root of a great deal of domestic violence. She told *Woman's Hour* that she was not a prohibitionist, but believed in encouraging temperance. 'No one thought I'd be re-elected when that was the subject of my maiden speech, but the people of Plymouth were brave. I stuck to Plymouth. Plymouth stuck to me.'

Nancy's majority was reduced in 1922 when the brewers ran an independent candidate against her, but she was returned on a further six occasions, only retiring, reluctantly, and at her husband's request, in 1945. Her most significant legislative achievement was the passing of a law in 1923 prohibiting the sale of alcohol to anyone under the age of eighteen. It was the first piece of legislation resulting from a Private Member's Bill brought by a woman MP.

She also campaigned on a variety of women's issues, including widows' pensions, employment rights, maternal mortality rates, nursery school provision and the raising of the age of consent. She was the only female MP until 1921 and she received up to two thousand letters each week from women asking for her help in raising their concerns.

Curiously, she opposed an equal divorce law, even though she was divorced. Her stance on the subject was one of a number of inconsistencies and was, perhaps, associated with her conversion to Christian Science, a belief system that suited her values of self-reliance and hard work. She did become something of a missionary for her faith and is reputed to have attempted to convert Stalin in 1931. Stalin was having none of it. She was not an entirely faithful adherent to the rules of her church as she is known to have sought medical advice when necessary. The press pilloried her for her opposition to equal divorce.

Nancy always stuck to her guns and was never afraid of the party whips:

> This was because women had put me in to represent them. I was concerned with women and children. I felt it was my duty to do it. I wanted the world to get better and it couldn't if it was gonna be ruled by men. I'm amazed how well they did it for two thousand years alone. We know what they are if we leave 'em in the house alone! Why did I have the courage to fight for what I believed in? Because I would tell 'em, I've got the women and you will hear from 'em. And so they did, didn't they? It's amazin' how well the men treated me, considerin' how few wanted me.

As the Second World War approached Nancy and her 'Cliveden Set' became known for their views on appeasement. It was not unusual for members of the aristocracy to oppose war with Germany. Indeed, there are questions over some members of the Royal Family having sympathy with Hitler, as did prominent members of the Mitford family and their high-powered associates. The American Ambassador, Joe Kennedy, was in the appeasement camp and would have been part of the Astors' social circle. Nancy made it clear that, having lived through the Great War, she was simply terrified of another such conflict.

She openly opposed communism and Catholicism, but there is no evidence that she was pro-Nazi, although, like a number of those in the appeasement movement, she had meetings with German officers. She spoke out against their treatment of women and the Nazi ideal of *Kinder, Küche, Kirche* – that women were only suited to attending church, having babies and cooking. At the start of the war she made an apology for having favoured appeasement and voted against Neville Chamberlain, but her reputation was damaged.

I guess in many ways Nancy Astor is best known for her verbal fencing with Winston Churchill, and she didn't always come away with a victory. She told Mr Churchill one evening in the House that he was drunk. He replied, 'And you, madam, are ugly, but tomorrow I shall be sober.' On another occasion she told him that if he were her husband she would poison his tea. To which Churchill replied, 'Madam, if you were my wife, I would drink it.'

When asked about her relationship with Churchill on *Woman's Hour* she talked about a social event where they had met and she had asked him why in her early days in the House he and his fellow MPs had never spoken to her. 'He told me they hoped to freeze me out. It felt, he said, like a woman had entered his bathroom and he had nothing to protect himself apart from his sponge. I told him he was not handsome enough to have such fears!'

Nancy's lasting legacy as an MP is that she quietly and conservatively wormed her way into the House of Commons, working within the sphere of women and children, and didn't frighten the horses. She was an effective model for those who came after her. She was quiet, rarely caused a ruckus, was of the same class as most of the male MPs and gave them a chance to get used to her and to the idea of women being a part of the parliamentary system. Her more forthright sisters followed on.

Nancy died in 1964, and her ashes were interred at the Octagon Temple at Cliveden. Some of her last words sum up the dry wit of the woman who blazed a trail for us all. During her final illness, at her daughter's home in Grimsthorpe Castle in Lincolnshire, her children gathered around her bed. 'Jakie,' she asked, 'is it my birthday, or am I dying?'

'I don't care if they call me the chairman,
the chairwoman, the chairperson or
the chair – *as long as I'm in the chair.*'

Barbara Castle

# 18

# Barbara Castle

## 1910–2002

There are two female politicians I would describe as the most exciting, sympathetic and forceful women I have ever met, and trying to choose which of them should appear in this book was the hardest task of all. Shirley Williams, now Baroness Williams, who retired from the House of Lords in 2016 at the age of eighty-five, has always been an honest, straight-talking politician who agonised over leaving the Labour Party to join the SDP, now the Liberal Democrats, but spent much of her political life fighting for women's rights, not only in this country but all over the world. Her intellect, sense of humour and clear thinking have always been a delight to hear and I once described her as having integrity stamped through her like a stick of Blackpool rock.

But, given only twenty-one women with whom to chart a history of Britain, I had to go for Barbara Castle because it was thanks to her that in 1975, in my mid-twenties, the principles of Equal Pay and Sex Discrimination were established in law. I had been trying to get a mortgage. I had the deposit. I earned enough to pay the monthly instalments. Every building society refused me without the signature of a husband or father. As the law changed, I was able to go back and threaten legal action if I didn't get the right to a mortgage without the backing of a man. It was

Barbara Castle who had spoken for women's rights in Parliament, drove her fellow MPs, still largely male, to find the political will to enshrine equality in law and inspired me to believe I could be an independent woman.

Barbara Anne Betts was born in Chesterfield on 6 October 1910, the youngest of the three children of Frank and Annie Betts. Her father was a tax inspector and moved around the north of England with his job. From Chesterfield they moved to Pontefract, then to Bradford and then, in 1931, to the town of Hyde in Greater Manchester. Her teenage years, from ten to nineteen, were spent in Bradford and I remember her telling me that she was proud to be a Yorkshirewoman, even though she'd been born in Derbyshire. It was, she reckoned, the root of her grit.

I met her for the first time in the mid-1970s when she came to be interviewed on the regional television programme I presented in Southampton. She was then Secretary of State for Health and Social Security and had a fearsome reputation as a fiery redhead who took no prisoners. She could not have been more charming. She shared my dressing room without complaint, whipped a fresh dress from her small suitcase, shook it out and put it on. 'Tricel, love,' she grinned, 'marvellous stuff. Shove it in your bag, shake it out, no ironing. You must learn to save labour in whatever way you can.' Politics and housekeeping in one easy joke.

We had the first of many long conversations that day as we waited for the programme to begin. Her love of smart clothes and the importance of a good hairdo (something she never shared with Shirley Williams, who didn't give a hoot about her hair) she inherited, she said, from her mother who'd earned her living as a milliner before becoming a Labour councillor.

But it was her father she talked about most. He'd made sure he could afford to send all three of his children, including the two girls, to fee-paying grammar schools in Bradford. As an egalitarian and active socialist, he believed a good education should be free to all children, but was determined, as it didn't exist at that time, that he would pay. He also believed that girls should have exactly the same opportunities as boys. A supportive father, she told me, was essential if a girl was going to get on.

In her autobiography, *Fighting All the Way*, she describes him as 'a forbidding presence with a violent temper and a cutting tongue'. She was aware that he was bitter that his well-off but mean father had refused to fund him to go to university and that whatever higher education he had came as a result of his own efforts without the help of teachers. He wrote poetry and remained a powerful influence on his daughter's political development. One of the saddest events in her life was his death in 1945 at the age of only sixty-three from Parkinson's Disease. It was four weeks before she was elected to the House of Commons, so he never saw her achieve her ambition.

Bradford was the city that formed young Barbara's political philosophy. It was there that the Independent Labour Party had been founded in 1893; Keir Hardie had fought a by-election there and the city went on to produce some of the Labour Party's first MPs. When Barbara was made head girl at the grammar school she stood as a Labour candidate in a mock general election, while her father, not allowed to engage in political activity as a civil servant, worked behind the scenes in the editorial department of the city's weekly socialist newspaper, *The Bradford Pioneer*.

Both Barbara and her elder sister, Marjorie, won places at St Hugh's College, Oxford. Barbara had won an exhibition worth £30, but seems to have found her time at university a terrible disappointment. Women were not allowed to speak in the Oxford Union and, while she won office in the Labour Club, it was at a low level, effectively doing secretarial work. She was surprisingly open in her autobiography and in conversation with me about her social life. She had lots of boyfriends, lost her virginity and did very little academic work, ending her time there with a third-class degree in Philosophy, Politics and Economics.

Barbara returned home, now in Hyde, terrified that her father would be furious at her lack of academic achievement. He, she told me, decided that Oxford had failed her rather than the other way around and, as she found it almost impossible to get the job in journalism she had hoped for – the local paper folded soon after she was offered a role there – he agreed to support her in working for the Labour Party.

She was full of stories about her early political career and often repeated her favourites in her typical dry, wry tone. Her father, for instance, had introduced her to the local party agent and she effectively became the party's propagandist, setting herself up on street corners in Hyde and other nearby towns and climbing up onto the back of a lorry or a soapbox to speak. 'Well,' she said, 'there was this morning and this fella got up onto the back of the lorry to introduce me. He was a right chauvinist and he shouted out "Now, ladies and gentlemen, we have a most extraordinary phenomenon, a woman wot speaks." And I did and I got better and better at it. That showed him!'

Barbara did eventually get a job, through a Labour contact, demonstrating and selling sweets in a department store, but her opportunity to advance her political career came when William Mellor, editor of the *Daily Herald* and a leading speaker on behalf of the Socialist League, addressed a meeting in Hyde that Barbara and her mother attended. Mrs Betts invited him to tea and Barbara would write, sixty years later in *Fighting All the Way*, 'Our mutual attraction was immediate.'

Mellor was twice Barbara's age and married with a young son. Their affair lasted until his death in 1942 and they were professionally connected as well. Mellor became the founding editor in 1937 of the fortnightly socialist newspaper *Tribune*. It was in *Tribune* that George Orwell wrote his 'As I Please' column for a number of years. Mellor hired Barbara to write about trade union matters, together with a young Michael Foot, who went on to lead the Labour Party from 1980 to 1983.

The affair was not a particularly satisfying one for Barbara. Mellor made numerous promises to leave his wife, but never did, and Barbara spent a great deal of time alone waiting for him to come and see her. The political journalist Anthony Howard, while accepting that she had to some degree been strung along by Mellor until her early thirties, wrote that 'it could be argued that the reward for all that was her eventual emergence as the woman with the most muscular cast of mind of any female politician of her generation'.

A year after Mellor's death Barbara met another married man, and he really was on the cusp of divorce. He was Ted Castle, the assistant editor of the *Daily Mirror*. Barbara was by now a St Pancras borough councillor and had been drafted into the Ministry of Food as an administrative officer early in the war. She was invited to speak at the 1943 Labour Party Conference in Central Hall Westminster about the Beveridge Report on Social Insurance and Allied Services. It would eventually be influential in establishing the welfare state and the National Health Service.

The unions were not keen on Beveridge's proposals for national insurance, which would be taken automatically from a worker's pay and used to fund health and welfare. Barbara rounded on the unions in her speech and told them that the world they stood for was one in which there would always be 'jam yesterday, jam tomorrow, but never jam today'. Her photo and the quotation were splashed across the *Mirror*'s front page. Ted Castle went to Central Hall the next day, invited her for a cup of coffee, offered her a job as a columnist and a year later they were married at the City of London register office. The reception was held at the Café Royal in Regent Street and Aneurin Bevan, the Minister for Health who led the foundation of the NHS, and his wife and fellow politician, Jennie Lee, were among the guests.

There's no doubt that the publicity her husband had given her in the *Mirror* was helpful when the women's section of the Blackburn Labour Party put her name forward as a prospective candidate for the 1945 general election. The selection committee interviewed her a few weeks before her wedding as Miss Barbara Betts. She was chosen and became the candidate as Mrs Barbara Castle.

It was the local agent who demanded it, saying, 'Here in Lancashire we don't like career women who persist in using their maiden names.' Barbara didn't make a fuss, and she thought Ted would be pleased. She revealed much later in her diaries that he had been jealous of her success and the extent to which politics took up the time he felt should be reserved for him. She was also, while sympathetic to feminism, never in the front line of championing the cause.

Indeed, when I interviewed her in 1993 on publication of *Fighting All the Way* she teased me about my commitment to the feminist project. 'You know, Jenni, sometimes I think you young feminists take it all a bit too far. I don't care if they call me the chairman, the chairwoman, the chairperson or the chair – *as long as I'm in the chair.*' Despite her apparent reluctance to be seen as the woman who took on women's issues, she did spend two years in the early 1960s trying to get charges at turnstiles in women's public toilets abolished. 'Why should women have to pay for a wee when men don't?' was her usual forthright opinion on the matter.

In July 1945 there was a surprising Labour landslide when Clement Attlee swept to power, overcoming Winston Churchill's Conservatives. Churchill had been the hero of the war, but the hostilities were over and the nation needed to be rebuilt. The Labour Party's campaign manifesto was entitled 'Let Us Face the Future' and promised full employment, a National Health Service that would be free at the point of need, and a welfare system that would take care of the population from 'cradle to grave'.

Of the 393 Labour MPs that were returned to Parliament, only twenty-three of them, including Mrs Castle, were women. At thirty-four, she became the youngest woman in the Commons. She served as parliamentary private secretary to Sir Stafford

Cripps, President of the Board of Trade, and later to Harold Wilson, with whom she developed a close working relationship. It was to prove a useful friendship later in her career.

She and Ted were keen to have children, but it never happened. She was, though, a loving and involved aunt to her sister's two daughters and son. When Marjorie died suddenly in 1964 Barbara became a mother figure for the children and later a 'grandmother' to their children.

Barbara developed a power base within the party by proving herself to be one of its most effective speakers and being sent around the country as one of the *Tribune* brains trusts, engaging the membership in debate and discussion. In 1950 she was elected through the women's section onto the National Executive Committee. A year later she decided to give up her women's seat and take her chance at one of seven seats chosen by the constituencies. No woman had ever achieved it. Barbara did.

As a woman on the left of the party she was not a favourite of the party leader Hugh Gaitskell, but when he died in 1963 and Harold Wilson took his place her prospects improved. In 1964 he became Prime Minister and Barbara was invited to join the Cabinet as Minister for Overseas Development. Her next job, quite surprising for a woman who never learned to drive, was Minister for Transport. She was responsible for the introduction of the breathalyser, and a law requiring seatbelts to be installed in all cars was passed in 1966. Abuse from the men who objected to a woman telling them how to drive poured down on her. She couldn't have cared less.

So effective was Barbara as a minister, Wilson described her as 'the best man in my Cabinet' and was determined to raise her even higher. She was not offered the job she wanted – Foreign Secretary – but in April 1968 he made her First Secretary of State and Secretary of State for Employment and Productivity.

She brought the government close to disaster when she introduced a White Paper called 'In Place of Strife'. The government had been dogged by a series of unofficial strikes and Wilson approved of her proposals to reform the trade unions. The unions did not, though, and neither did the parliamentary Labour Party, many of whose members were funded by the unions. She and Wilson limped on together, pretending that they had managed to get concessions from the Trades Union Congress. It's generally accepted that Castle was right in what she was trying to do, but her timing was misguided.

Most people thought her reputation would never recover, but she fought back with the Equal Pay Act, which was the last piece of legislation to reach the statute book in 1970 before the Labour government was defeated at the general election. Her determination to right the wrong of unequal pay had begun early in her career. She told me how appalled she'd been when, as a young MP, she saw the pay scales at companies in her constituency. The Castle eyes flashed and the voice rose a decibel or two as she explained what she discovered. 'The blooming bosses would put these sheets of paper in front of me with a printed-out pay scale. And they were proud of it. At the top was Managerial, then Skilled, then Unskilled, then Women. Right at the bottom, as if that were perfectly acceptable. I determined even then that I would do something about it.'

It was the Ford sewing machinists' strike in Dagenham in 1968 that gave her the opportunity to act. The women demanded to be paid the same as similarly skilled men and the leaders of the strike asked Mrs Castle to intervene on their behalf with the management. She helped them win a pay rise that brought them up to ninety-two per cent of what the men earned. Not quite equal, but a significant rise. The Equal Pay Act that she steered through Parliament received Royal Assent in 1970, but didn't come into force until December 1975 at the same time as the Sex Discrimination Act.

In opposition in the early 1970s she was shadow Secretary of State for Health and Social Services, and when Labour won the

'74 election she carried that job into the last Wilson Cabinet. She improved pension provision, introducing the rule that pensions should rise in line with average earnings, introduced disability benefits and changed Child Benefit. It wasn't right, she thought, that it should be paid to fathers who might not make sure it went to the children. Instead it should go to the mother. She called it a transfer from the wallet to the purse.

When James Callaghan succeeded Harold Wilson as Prime Minister, Barbara Castle's face no longer fitted. She told me once that when Callaghan, a bitter political enemy of hers, told her he wanted someone younger in the Cabinet she'd been tempted to tell him to look to himself. Callaghan was four years older than Wilson. She didn't say it and told me it was the most restrained thing she'd ever done in her life. Callaghan sacked her and in 1979 she resigned her seat. Ted Castle, ennobled by Harold Wilson, died at home on Boxing Day 1979. Barbara had to keep busy.

During the 1975 European referendum she had voted against Britain remaining part of the European Economic Community, but no sooner had she left Westminster than she put herself forward for the European Parliament. Her reason for standing in Greater Manchester North in 1979, she said, was because 'politics is not just about policies. It is about fighting for them in every available forum and at every opportunity.' She was an MEP until 1989.

In 1990 she accepted a peerage and became Baroness Castle of Blackburn. She was lonely and bored and took the life peerage simply as a way of remaining active in politics. With few other interests, she did her job in the Lords with her usual diligence and was particularly active in fighting for pensioners' rights. In 1999 she tore Labour ministers limb from limb when they fixed pension increases to the rate of inflation rather than average earnings. At the Party Conference in Bournemouth she made a furious speech:

'This means a pension increase of 72p – a fair price for a bag of peanuts.'

Barbara died on 3 May 2002 at her home in Buckinghamshire, having fought for what she believed in to the very end. I loved 'The Red Queen', as she was known, and I still miss those days when she breezed gaily into my studio and spoke with such passion and humour.

Anthony Howard wrote an assessment of her legacy that I really can't better.

Her real memorial lies perhaps in the fact that in her lifetime Britain had a woman prime minister. Without Barbara Castle, it is doubtful if Margaret Thatcher would ever have got to Downing Street. By taking on men on equal terms and refusing to be patronized or even flattered by them, Castle did not merely banish the always rather bogus age of chivalry from politics. She also blazed a trail for others to follow – in a way that no previous female politician had managed to do.

'I am not a woman Prime Minister,
I am a Prime Minister.'

Margaret Thatcher

# 19

# Margaret Thatcher

## 1925–2013

People often ask me whether I'm ever nervous when I have to interview someone famous. Of course, there's always that slight flutter of apprehension no matter who the interviewee is going to be, whether they're famous or not. You want to get it right. I've always said the day the nerves go away will be the day I have to acknowledge I've become dangerously over-confident and complacent.

I do, though, have to admit that only one interviewee in my entire career has absolutely terrified me. And that was Margaret Thatcher. She had the most piercing blue eyes that drove right through you once she had you in her critical sights. It always started well: the welcome when you arrived at Downing Street to speak to her was warm, her voice was soft and caressing . . . but you knew you were face to face with an extremely dangerous creature. At any moment the fangs could be bared as she spotted a weakness in your research, a little lack of knowledge or under-standing, and it seemed to delight her to tear you apart.

The first time I met Margaret Thatcher was in 1979, soon after the May general election in which the country bubbled over with the extremes of either delight or dismay at the fact that it had really happened. We had a *woman* Prime Minister. I was naturally disposed to dislike her. She looked like the kind of woman my mother had wanted me to be. Her clothes were immaculate and often exaggeratedly feminine. Her hair and make-up were perfect. She even wore hats, twinsets, pearls and diamond brooches. She had not been touched by the fashion revolution of the 1960s and I had found myself torn in two on the day of her ascendance from her home in Flood Street in Chelsea to Number 10.

I had found her speech – quoting St Francis of Assisi – smarmy and nauseating: 'Where there is discord, may we bring harmony. Where there is error, may we bring truth. Where there is doubt, may we bring faith and where there is despair, may we bring hope.' But she was a woman! And she was the Prime Minister! And that was the most extraordinarily exciting thing imaginable. Like so many others, I would spend the next eleven years loving her and loathing her.

One of the foundations of Thatcher's political philosophy was the belief that the state should stand back and let the individual become self-reliant, and her first journey into the southern region where I was a young television reporter took her to Salisbury, where she would hand over the keys to a family who were buying their council house. The Right to Buy was enshrined in law in the Housing Act the following year.

I had never seen such a crush of people turn out to see a politician. The streets of Salisbury resembled what we would now expect to see in an American presidential election – hundreds of people cheering and calling out her name in a most un-British manner. She began the day at the council house, toured the city, went to the Wilton carpet factory and other small businesses around the area, and towards the end of the afternoon, I, a mere twenty-nine-year-old, was flagging rather desperately and she, at fifty-four, looked as cool, fresh and energetic as she had first thing.

At one point in the late afternoon the crowd trying to get close to her was so pressing she was surrounded by half a dozen huge, burly policemen. I had lost my cameraman and sound recordist in the melee, but I'd managed to stay close to the leading lady. I found myself being squeezed painfully between her fans and her police protectors. A hand popped out from behind the coppers. It grabbed mine and pulled me into the circle.

'Come along, dear,' she smiled. 'Stay by me. We don't want a talented young journalist to be squashed to death, do we?' We chatted for a while about her phenomenal reception, her children, the twins Mark and Carol, then in their mid-twenties – she said she thought they might find it difficult being thrust to such a great degree into the public eye – the fact that her husband Denis had dipped out of the trip around lunchtime and was probably enjoying a drink somewhere safe, and then, as we arrived at the next venue, she shook my hand, wished me luck and said, 'Goodbye, dear. I'm sure we'll meet again.' I was quite bowled over and furious that I'd had no way of recording our conversation.

Margaret Roberts was born in 1925, the daughter of a devout Methodist grocer in Grantham in Lincolnshire, Alfred Roberts, and his wife, Beatrice. She adored her austere father and learned from him her principles of hard work and public service. We know virtually nothing about her mother. She was not even mentioned in Margaret's entry in *Who's Who* or the first volume of her autobiography. She told an interviewer for the *Daily Express* in 1961 that she had loved her mother dearly 'but after I was fifteen we had nothing more to say to each other'. Her older sister, Muriel, never gets a mention either.

Her life as a child was simple. The family lived in the flat above the shop and Margaret helped her father run the business, learned how to manage money with great care, understood the basics of trade and began to develop her political instincts. There was nothing of the rich Tory grandee about her background. She was the kind of Conservative – her father was a councillor – who believed in pulling yourself up by your bootstraps, knowing what you want to achieve and working hard to get there, regardless of your class background.

A recent revelation about Margaret Thatcher, in a book about Ronald Reagan and her close relationship with the American president, refers to her nervousness as a public speaker. She told the author, James Rosenbush, 'You never completely lose the fear, no, never. Sometimes when I reach the podium I say to myself, "Come on, old gal, you can do it." But that little bit of fear always sticks with you, and the energy you derive from it gives you more courage to press onward with what you have to say.'

Her self-belief was legendary and was clearly there in her early life. At junior school in Grantham at the age of nine she won a prize and was congratulated on her good luck. 'I wasn't lucky,' she said, 'I deserved it.'

Margaret won a scholarship to Kesteven and Grantham Girls' School and her school reports show a hard-working girl determined to keep on improving. She became head girl in 1942 and in the Upper Sixth applied for a scholarship to study Chemistry at Somerville College, Oxford. She was rejected, but was offered a place after another girl withdrew.

She studied X-Ray crystallography under the Nobel Prize winner Dorothy Hodgkin and her subject for dissertation was the structure of the antibiotic gramicidin. She graduated in 1947 with a second-class degree. She had not, though, neglected her politics. She became President of the Oxford University Conservative Association in 1946 and began to read books such as Friedrich Hayek's *The Road to Serfdom*. He was the great free-market thinker and warned, in his book, that the dead hand of the bureaucrat could threaten a free society almost as much as the iron boot of Stalin. In a BBC television programme about Hayek, Lord Patten said that Thatcher would often pull favourite Hayek quotations from her handbag at key moments during Cabinet meetings.

Margaret's first job was in Colchester at BX Plastics where she was hired as a research chemist. In 1948 she applied for a job at

ICI, but she was rejected. The personnel department's assessment of the young chemist was: 'This woman is headstrong,
obstinate and dangerously self-opinionated.'

Margaret joined the local Conservative Association and
attended the Party Conference in 1948, where she met an old
Oxford friend who told her Dartford in Kent were looking for
candidates. The headstrong, obstinate woman impressed the
selection committee and, at twenty-four, she was the youngest
female Conservative candidate, attracting a good deal of media
attention. In Dartford she supported herself with a job at J. Lyons
and Co. developing emulsifiers for ice cream, but it was a safe
Labour seat and she failed to get elected.

But in 1949 she found the man who would take away all her
worries about earning a living and remain a silent support
throughout her political career. She had met Denis Thatcher at a
dinner to mark her formal adoption as the Dartford candidate.
He was a divorced, wealthy, successful businessman who lived by
a mantra he had learned from his father: 'It is better to keep your
mouth shut and be thought a fool than to open it and remove all
doubt.' They married two years after their first meeting.

Denis Thatcher brought his new wife many gifts. His income
funded her training as a barrister and she would always talk
proudly of what a perfect grounding her education had been for
a successful world leader – science and the law. He bought a house
in fashionable Chelsea and another in the country and after the
twins were born in 1953 she had no worries about finding good-
quality childcare. She had some difficulty finding a safer seat than
Dartford, as a number of Conservative committees would not
accept that a young mother could run for Parliament. Her
response was to make public her view that she hoped we would
see more and more women combining marriage and a career.

It was in this field that so many young feminists who had been
delighted by Thatcher's rise to the top of British politics found
themselves infuriated by her. She never, in all her time as Prime

Minister, gave any other women a hand up into the Cabinet. Her only female appointment was Baroness Janet Young – a member of the House of Lords and not an elected politician. When asked about this omission she would always argue that the time would come, but none of the young Conservative MPs were ready yet. She never hesitated to gather attractive young men around her – experienced or otherwise.

On the childcare question – the one difficulty faced by all women who want a family and a career – she was extremely unsympathetic. In an interview with me in the mid-1980s she railed about 'countries like Russia where I've seen poor, pale, tiny little children being dragged along to a crèche in the early morning and forced to spend the day away from their home. No. No. No.' She recommended that an ambitious woman with children should 'find herself a little part-time job to keep her mind active and a lovely aunt or grandmother to care for her children for a few hours a week'. No joy there for those women desperate for childcare they could rely on and could afford, which would enable them to do the kind of full-time job Margaret Thatcher enjoyed.

Her children were only six when she finally became a candidate for a safe parliamentary seat, but, if a drama documentary, *Margaret Thatcher: The Long Walk to Finchley*, broadcast in 2008, is to be believed, she found them useful in fulfilling her ambition of getting selected. Several selection committees who had preferred a war hero to a young woman had rejected her, but with Denis' help she began to use what the old boy network had perceived as her weakness – her sex. She portrayed herself as a woman who understood the concerns of the nuclear family – she had one – and, on Denis' advice, dyed her hair blonde and perfected her flirtatious manner. She managed to appeal to both the men and the women on the committee in the safe Conservative seat of Finchley in north London and in 1959 was elected as their MP.

\* \* \*

Thatcher's rise through Harold Macmillan's government was speedy. By 1961 she was Parliamentary Undersecretary for Pensions and National Insurance and after Labour won in 1964 she held a number of shadow ministerial positions. She voted in favour of two of the most controversial issues of the time – decriminalising homosexuality and abortion – but she voted to retain capital punishment.

In 1970 the Conservatives came back into power with Ted Heath as their leader and he appointed Margaret Thatcher Minister for Education. Willie Whitelaw, then Leader of the House, is said to have warned Heath, 'Once she's there we'll never get rid of her,' and it would not be long before Heath and Thatcher developed a deep loathing of each other.

Her time as Education Secretary saw her make one of the biggest and best-remembered mistakes of her career. As part of her cuts to the education budget she ended the provision of a bottle of free milk for every primary school child. This earned her the title 'Thatcher, Thatcher, milk snatcher', and she later said it had been a valuable lesson. She had 'incurred the maximum of political odium for the minimum of political benefit'.

She had been talked about as a possible future Prime Minister since the early 1960s, but in 1970 Margaret declared, 'There will not be a woman Prime Minister in my lifetime – the male population is too prejudiced.' A mere four years later, when the Tories lost the 1974 election, she stood against Edward Heath for leadership of the party. She was seen as a right-wing outsider, but she knew how to galvanise backbenchers with her forceful style and how to win friends with her charm in the tearooms of the Commons. She became the leader in 1975, quickly moving the party to the right, together with her close friend and colleague Keith Joseph – a keen advocate of free-market conservatism and reducing the power of the unions.

In 1979 the Conservatives swept to power after a Labour term that had been wracked by industrial unrest and the 'Winter of

Discontent'. Her advertising campaign was catchlined 'Labour Isn't Working', and she sold herself as the practical housewife who knew how to balance a budget, and who could be trusted to sort out the nation's shambolic economy.

For the next eleven years the woman with the carefully trained voice and immaculate appearance bestrode Britain like a colossus. She sacked the 'wets' – the politicians who leaned towards the more liberal side of the Tory Party – from her Cabinet, together with the grandees she said had treated her like their cleaning lady, and surrounded herself with like-minded monetarists. When the country fell into recession her critics demanded a U-turn. She hit back with: 'You turn if you want to. The lady's not for turning.' Inflation was not brought under control, high interest rates terrified those of us with mortgages to pay, unemployment rose to two million and riots broke out in London and Liverpool.

The polls had her down as the most unpopular Prime Minister since records began and defeat seemed certain. And then, in April 1982, Argentina invaded the British-run Falkland Islands. The Foreign Office wanted a peaceful settlement, but Thatcher became positively Churchillian and sent troops to the South Atlantic within days.

After ten days of fighting the Falklands were retaken. Although 649 Argentinians and 255 British soldiers and sailors died, Thatcher's response to the conflict seemed cold as she was photographed on a tank, the conquering hero, and said, 'When you've spent half your political life dealing with humdrum issues like the environment, it's exciting to have a real crisis on your hands.' 'The Iron Lady' was born and her popularity rocketed.

She romped through the 1983 election and the 'loadsamoney' culture began to take hold. Council houses were bought, shares in British Gas, British Rail and British Telecommunications sold like hot cakes as the utilities were privatised and financial institutions in the City were deregulated. The economy boomed, but inequality and homelessness increased. The economic free-for-all would prove disastrous in the long term.

For me, a girl from Barnsley whose grandfathers had worked at the pit all their lives, the Miners' Strike, which began in 1984, was a painful and deeply upsetting period. I was sent by *Newsnight* to cover the soup kitchen set up by Anne Scargill, the wife of the leader of the miners. I stood in the early morning filming the pickets outside my maternal grandfather's colliery as they sang 'We Shall Overcome' and watched the community in which I'd been raised crumble as its only major industry died. Thatcher never bowed under the pressure. She wounded the power of the unions, and in the working-class community I come from you simply don't mention her name.

It was during the 1984 Conservative Party Conference in Brighton that you saw the true nature of the Iron Lady. The IRA bomb, which went off in the Grand Hotel, nearly killed her and her husband. Five people died and thirty-four were injured, but the next morning, seemingly unruffled, she stood up and made her speech, condemning the bombers and stating quite clearly that 'this attack has failed. All attempts to destroy democracy by terrorism will fail.'

When I met her in the late 1980s it became clear to me that she had become too much of a believer in her own publicity and had convinced herself that her bringing together of Reagan and Gorbachev was sorting out all the problems of the world. She had, she told me, been able to do business with Gorbachev – they had met at Chequers in 1984 – and she had a long and close relationship with President Reagan. She had engineered a meeting between the two leaders in Geneva in November 1985 to discuss bilateral nuclear arms reductions, and Reagan and Gorbachev met again at the Reykjavik summit in Iceland in 1986 that aimed to revive the discussions. She had, undoubtedly, achieved important negotiations between the world's two most powerful men. It did, though, seem something of an exaggeration when she claimed sole responsibility for the end of the Cold War, presenting the reunification of Germany and the break-up of the Soviet Union as entirely her own work.

Thatcher also insisted that the poll tax was a brilliant idea of hers. In 1987 local council rates were abolished and a flat rate community charge was introduced as a local tax, which everyone would pay regardless of their income. There were riots and marches across the country with people carrying banners saying 'Can't Pay, Won't Pay'. Thatcher refused to back down.

It was the beginning of the end as the poll tax and disputes over Europe – she was vehemently opposed to any idea of a European Superstate – lost her support within the party. There's also evidence that the charming woman who had seduced her colleagues in the tearooms in the early days had become imperious and rude, even to her closest supporters. It was Sir Geoffrey Howe, her Deputy PM and former Chancellor of the Exchequer and Foreign Secretary, who delivered the death blow.

Howe was a keen pro-European and opposed Thatcher's handling of the government's relationship with the European Community. In his resignation speech on 13 November 1990, believed to have been written by his doughty wife, Elspeth, he accused the Prime Minister of 'sending your opening batsmen to the crease, only for them to find, as the first balls are being bowled, that their bats have been broken before the game by the team captain'. He ended with, 'The time has come for others to consider their own response to the tragic conflict of loyalties with which I have myself wrestled for perhaps too long.' A fortnight later we saw her weep as she left Downing Street with Denis on 28 November 1990.

The last time I interviewed Margaret Thatcher was when she published her autobiography, *The Downing Street Years*, in 1993. She agreed to come to the studio – my territory rather than hers – and I thought, here was my chance to ask her to explain how constant references to her gender throughout her political career had affected her. She had always batted such questions aside in the past and invariably said to me and to other journalists, 'I am not a woman Prime Minister, I am a Prime Minister.'

I genuinely thought I might persuade her to discuss, for the benefit of other women who might want to enter politics, how she dealt with those Cabinet ministers who had treated her like the cleaning lady. I formulated a question that went, 'How did you deal with the Tory grandees who couldn't treat a woman as an equal and the constant references to you handbagging wrong-doers – no one ever says a man has briefcased someone? Then there was Alan Clark writing in his diaries how much he had lusted during Prime Minister's Questions over your finely turned ankles, or President Mitterrand saying you had the eyes of Caligula and the lips of Marilyn Monroe?'

The following weekend the radio critic of the *Sunday Times* said it was the only time ever his radio had frozen over. A tough moment for me. There is nothing more alarming for an interviewer than an interviewee who says absolutely nothing. I moved on quickly to another question and only realised much later that these were things she had never heard before. Her highly protective press secretary, Bernard Ingham, presented her with cuttings from the newspapers and kept from her everything he felt she didn't need to know.

Margaret Thatcher became a Baroness in 1992 and was politically active in the Lords until, when Denis died in 2003, her attendance became more infrequent. In 2007 her statue was placed in the Houses of Parliament opposite her hero, Winston Churchill, and in 2013, at the age of eighty-seven, she died. She was given a ceremonial funeral with full military honours. Some people wept for her; others sang 'Ding! Dong! The witch is dead'. She was loved and loathed in equal measure to the end.

What remains is Thatcherism. In 2016, the former Prime Minister David Cameron said, 'We are all Thatcherites.' Thatcher's political philosophy has shaped the nation in a way no other has. Privatisation of essential services, the reduction in public housing, the free market, deregulation of financial services and a culture where a person is expected to stand on their own two feet. The state we're in was shaped by her.

But she did make an extraordinary step forward for women. Shirley Williams told me once that she was most grateful to Thatcher for showing a woman was perfectly capable of engaging her brain throughout her menopause.

After Thatcher was deposed, my older son, Ed, and I were in the kitchen, preparing supper, when it was announced on the radio that John Major would be the next Prime Minister.

'Mum,' said Ed, then aged seven, 'did they say John Major will be Prime Minister?'

'Yes,' I replied. 'That's right.'

He thought for a moment, looking puzzled. 'But, Mum, I thought that was a woman's job!'

'But I love vulgarity. Good taste
is death. Vulgarity is life.'

Mary Quant

# 20

# Mary Quant

## 1934–

The period I call the gender-quake, where everything began to change for women in Britain and the world as it used to be was turned upside down, started for me around 1964. I was far too young to be worrying about the arrival of the contraceptive pill, although of course it played a huge part in the liberation of millions of us, but I was just the right age to want to be Mary Quant.

My mother was in the Margaret Thatcher school of fashion, insisting I wear a bra, although I barely needed one, and a Playtex girdle – also unnecessary in those days. My hair was home-permed by my mum with a Twink solution. I had stockings and a suspender belt, a skirt that came, respectably, just below the knee, a buttoned-up blouse or twinset and, yes, even a string of pearls. The shoes had heels and were impossible to walk in, let alone run.

And then came Quant. She was born in Blackheath in London in 1934 to Welsh parents who both came from mining families. Jack and Mary had been awarded scholarships to grammar school, met at Cardiff University where they both came away with first-class degrees, trained as teachers and moved to London to work. Mary junior went to Blackheath High School and then studied illustration at Goldsmiths College. Her parents, she said in her book *Quant on Quant*, made it absolutely clear to her and her brother that they would have to earn their own living.

'My parents never even considered the possibility that marriage might be a way out for girls. I was made terribly aware that it was entirely my own responsibility to make a success of my life.' She left Goldsmiths with a diploma in art education and she began an apprenticeship at Erik, a high-class Mayfair milliner on Brook Street, next door to Claridge's.

As a child, immediately after the war and in the early 1950s, Mary was obsessed with fashion and says in her autobiography that she would generally inherit old clothes that she considered 'weren't really her'. In order to have the clothes she wanted she would make her own, even, on occasion, cutting up old bed sheets. With the skills from her training in millinery she quickly began designing and making garments with professional knowledge. The fashion business was an obvious career for her.

She had met Alexander Plunket Greene at Goldsmiths and they married in 1957. She described him to me as a cross between Mick Jagger and Paul McCartney, the best dancer that ever was and a terrific looker. She was besotted with him throughout his life.

In 1955 he inherited £5,000 and, together with a solicitor and photographer friend, Archie McNair, helped Mary open a boutique in the King's Road called Bazaar. The shop was above a basement restaurant called Alexander's, run by Plunket Greene. Her bestselling items in those early days were white plastic collars used to brighten up black dresses, t-shirts, men's cardigans worn as dresses, black stretch leggings and a pair of 'mad' (her term) lounging pyjamas made by Quant and featured in the fashion magazine *Harper's Bazaar*.

In her quest for new and interesting clothes for the shop she felt the range of gear available on the wholesale market was inadequate and decided to design and make all the stock herself. Tight skinny-rib sweaters, the wet-look clothes made of PVC and knee-high plastic boots came to be known as the 'London Look'. She was at the epicentre of sixties cool, defining 'mod' and hanging out on the King's Road with a roll call of the glamorous, rich and famous who were dragging the UK out from the shadows of postwar austerity and creating a new pop culture.

Life, she told me, became an endless party. She and APG, as she calls him, were so well connected they were invited in 1960 to the wedding of Princess Margaret and Anthony Armstrong-Jones and it was Armstrong-Jones who photographed her wet-look collection. Snobbery, she said, had gone out of fashion.

Bazaar's window displays screamed 'youth' and 'affordable', and Quant's trendy fashion shows drew masses of attention from the fashion magazines. In 1963 she won the Dress of the Year Award and in 1966 was awarded the OBE for her contribution to fashion.

Not everyone loved the look. Mary remembers bowler-hatted men rapping on the window at Bazaar to complain and shout out that her ideas were vulgar. A previous generation, she thinks, was terrified of change, but she didn't care. In 1967 she told a *Guardian* reporter, 'But I love vulgarity. Good taste is death. Vulgarity is life.' Models such as Jean Shrimpton and Twiggy, so different from the aristocratic-looking models of the 1940s and '50s, were skinny, leggy and gamine and, wearing Quant's clothes, began to define the shocking, sexually liberated, fun Chelsea Girl of Swinging London.

Quant's clothes were such an immediate success that in 1961 she opened the second Bazaar in Knightsbridge, designed by Terence Conran. When the lounging pyjamas were spotted and copied by an American manufacturer, J. C. Penney, Quant went global. Initially she worked alone, making up her designs herself in her flat, and then she employed a few machinists. By 1963 she was exporting to the US and by 1966 she was working with eighteen manufacturers.

*     *     *

Mary Quant revolutionised the fashion industry. The way fashion had been created before Quant was by dressmakers or couture houses, mostly based in Paris. Very few people could afford high-end fashion and most of those who wanted the current look would buy a pattern, take their measurements to a local dressmaker and have the piece made up or make it at home. Mary introduced the idea of buying your stylish stuff off the peg. She also, in a male-dominated fashion world, was a great entrepreneurial success once she and Alexander worked out how to price their clothes to make a profit. At the beginning they had made everything so cheap they lost a lot of cash.

She had one great advantage over previously established designers such as Chanel or Dior. She was a contemporary of her customers and understood exactly what they wanted. There has been some debate about whether or not it was Mary who actually invented the miniskirt. Some say it was the French designer Courrèges, but Mary told me herself that her inspiration for the look had been a girl she saw in a tap dance class dressed all in black with the shortest of skirts, black tights and white ankle socks. The real credit, though, she claimed, should go to her customers:

> It was the girls on the King's Road who invented the mini. I was making easy, youthful, simple clothes in which you could move, in which you could run and jump and we would make them the length the customer wanted. I wore them very short and the customers would say 'shorter, shorter!'

Quant dubbed the skirt the mini after her favourite car, the Mini, designed for the British Motor Corporation by Sir Alec Issigonis and first produced in 1959, and she defined the woman who wore it as 'curiously feminine, but their femininity lies in their attitude rather than their appearance . . . She enjoys being noticed, but wittily. She is lively, positive, opinionated.'

It was Jean Shrimpton, The Shrimp, who helped launch the miniskirt worldwide. In 1965 she made a two-week promotional visit to Melbourne and attended the races wearing a white shift that ended 3.9 inches above her knee. She wore no hat, stockings or gloves and had a man's watch. How our young lives were changed!

It wasn't just the clothes that Mary revolutionised. As the 1960s progressed she approached Vidal Sassoon to join with her in defining the new look of the liberated, uncluttered woman of the time and together they made everyone want his bob. She still wears her hair in exactly the same style. Then there were the bras – shaped naturally with no hard wiring. She spent a lot of time convincing the men who dominated the underwear industry how a comfortable bra should be designed and claims responsibility for introducing tights to the United States. Comfort was always her aim.

Her husband, who never needed to be persuaded of Mary's accurate judgement when it came to design and colour, was the PR talent in the family. He thought up the name Booby Traps for the bras. He was also responsible for the naming of items in the cosmetic range with her distinctive daisy logo, such as the range of lipstick called Jelly Babies and Jeepers Peepers mascara.

Her impact on the cosmetic industry was huge, but men working in the industry often had difficulty following her thinking. Why, they would ask, do women need a waterproof mascara? It seems so obvious, but it was Mary who told them that women swim and sometimes they cry. Streaks of mascara down a teary face is not an attractive look, she would tell them! She showed male executives how make-up is used and she brought male demonstrators into cosmetics departments – a massive change from when severe middle-aged ladies demonstrated to other severe middle-aged ladies.

The great tragedy of Mary's life was the death of Alexander Plunket Greene in 1990 at the age of only fifty-seven. She and their son, Orlando, born in 1970, adored him, but he had long been a bon viveur and in 1988 he had been told he would only have two years to live unless he stopped drinking. He didn't. Mary described their marriage as riotous. Her husband was 'a monstrous womaniser, so it was noisy and bumpy. We had great battles about it . . . It was wonderful, though. He was loyal at the same time, though. Unfaithful, but loyal. There was unhappiness, but a great deal of happiness too.'

Alexander is now gone and so too have Mary's rights to her name. It's been sold to a Japanese company that manufactures clothes and cosmetics under her trademark, but at the age of eighty-two she is still Mary Quant. She still diets – it's hard work to stay skinny, she says, and she's been on a diet since 1962 – and Dame Mary Quant, awarded her DBE in 2015, still gets her hair cut at a Vidal Sassoon salon in Chelsea.

Mary Quant's influence on the way British women looked and moved is incalculable. Ernestine Carter, an influential fashion journalist of the 1950s and '60s, wrote, 'It is given to a fortunate few to be born at the right time, in the right place, with the right talents. In recent fashion there are three: Chanel, Dior and Mary Quant.'

Mary Quant truly changed the lives of my generation of women in Britain and around the world by freeing us from the constraints of fashion, and her influence remains. I no longer wear a miniskirt, but lots of younger and some older women still do. My mother hated the 'London Look' and banned me from wearing 'an extended belt, those dark tights and that horrible black eye make-up and white lipstick'. But I still have the one I saved up to buy in 1965 (it no longer fits) and had to wear in secret, leaving it at my friend's house and changing in the toilets in Barnsley bus station for a Saturday evening out.

My friend looked after the make-up as well as the skirt and the skinny-rib sweater. The make-up had to be scrubbed off in the loo before I went home, but we thought we were the bees' knees as we strode across town – thoroughly modern Ms's.

And today, all these years later and not nearly so skinny as I was then? Thank you, Mary Quant, for bringing us tights and black leggings and Chelsea boots. My wardrobe, freedom of movement, confidence and, I guess, liberation, and that of so many of us, would be poorer even now without your genius.

'The most dangerous woman in Britain.'

The *Daily Mail*

# 21

# Nicola Sturgeon

## 1970–

Nicola Sturgeon's mother, Joan, said of her daughter, 'She's always been very driven. Nicola will always achieve what she wants to achieve.' Her rise to prominence during the 2015 general election showed her mother to be an accurate predictor of the future. Sturgeon had burst onto the British political scene as the new leader of the Scottish National Party and First Minister in the Scottish Parliament.

She had taken over the party in September 2014, following the result of the Scottish referendum on independence. The turnout had been phenomenal at eighty-five per cent, but the result had been a disappointment to the SNP: 55.3% voted against independence and 44.7% in favour. The former First Minister, Alex Salmond, stood down and a few days later Nicola announced her bid for the leadership.

In her speech she said:

> I believe as strongly today as I did last week that independence is the best future for Scotland and I am more convinced than ever that we will become an independent country . . . So my task will be to lead Scotland into an exciting new chapter in our national story . . . I also hope that my candidacy, should it succeed, will send a strong message to

every girl and young woman in Scotland. No matter your background or what you want to achieve in life, in Scotland 2014 there is no glass ceiling on ambition.

She won the election unopposed and became the first woman to lead her party and her country. Her eight-year-old niece, Harriet, was with her family as her aunt assumed office and Sturgeon said:

Harriet doesn't yet know about the gender pay gap or under-representation or the barriers like high childcare costs that make it so hard for so many women to work and pursue careers. My fervent hope is that she never will, that by the time she is a young woman she will have no need to know about any of these issues because they will have been consigned to history.

She made a determined start with her feminist ideas. Her Cabinet was announced on 21 November and had a fifty-fifty gender balance. And she was clearly doing something right for Scotland. By March 2015, SNP membership had risen to more than 102,000, a four-fold increase since the referendum only six months earlier. The SNP was now the third-largest party in Britain.

Sturgeon's general election campaign called for opposition to the coalition government's policies of austerity, restoration of the fifty pence tax band, full fiscal responsibility for the Scottish government at Holyrood, the abandonment of plans to build Trident and the abolition of the House of Lords.

The impression she made when she appeared on various television debates, both in Scotland and across the UK, was phenomenal. After one of the Leaders' Debates people across Britain were googling 'Can I vote for Nicola Sturgeon?', although some of the papers gave her a hard time. The *Sun* called her 'The Scotweiler.' *The Times* said she was 'the defining figure of the election campaign, as she tours the country in her 6in heels and bright suits, posing for selfies with adoring fans'. The *Daily Mail* dubbed her 'the most dangerous woman in Britain', to which she responded, 'It was the nicest thing the *Daily Mail* has ever said about me.'

Iain Macwhirter, in his book *Tsunami: Scotland's Democratic Revolution*, writes:

> Sharp, intelligent, confident, down to earth: Nicola Sturgeon's image chimed with how modern Scots like to regard themselves.
>
> Unionist newspapers had to swallow their loathing of the SNP and put her on the front pages day after day because she was simply so popular with their readers. Here was powerful Nicola in her smart red dress at her manifesto launch; smiling Nicola taking selfies with nice old ladies; exercising in a gymnasium; and grinning with small children in a Wendy House. 'Nicola', as everyone calls her in Scotland, has the gift of being able to convey a political message simply by being there.

As First Minister of Scotland's devolved Parliament, Nicola was not standing in the general election for the UK Parliament, but her party won all but three of the available seats in Scotland. The SNP swept the board from the Highlands to the Lowlands and from middle-class Edinburgh to working-class Glasgow. It was generally agreed it was the new party leader who had made the difference.

Nicola Sturgeon was born on 19 July 1970 in Irvine on the coast of the Firth of Clyde in North Ayrshire, a month after Ted Heath's Conservative Party won the general election and the SNP returned its first member to Westminster. Her parents, Robert and Joan, were very young, twenty-one and seventeen, when she came along and her sister, Gillian, was born five years later. Their mother stayed home to look after the girls and her father was an electrician. She's said she remembers her childhood as being one of total security and being entirely at one with the world around her.

Nicola went to secondary school at Greenwood Academy, close to her home, which was now in Dreghorn, between Irvine and Kilmarnock. It was at school that her interest in politics was awakened by her Modern Studies teacher. Her English teacher was also an influence. He was a Labour councillor who knew she was interested in politics and was so sure she would join the Labour Party he brought her a membership application without even asking. Apparently she said to herself, 'Stuff you! I'm going to join the SNP.'

Her motivation seems to have been Margaret Thatcher, who was Prime Minister at the time. She later said of Thatcher: 'I hated everything she stood for. This was the genesis of my nationalism.' In an interview Nicola gave to *Woman's Hour* in 2013, she recalled that:

> I joined the SNP when I was still at school . . . The economy wasn't in great shape, lots of people around me were looking at a life or an immediate future of unemployment and I think that certainly gave me a strong sense of social justice and, at that stage, a strong feeling that it was wrong for Scotland to be governed by a Tory government that we hadn't elected.

Not long before this, in a keynote speech delivered during the campaign for Scottish independence, she had addressed the oft-asked question of why she had joined the SNP rather than Labour: 'I joined the SNP because it was obvious to me then – as it still is today – that you cannot guarantee social justice unless you are in control of the delivery.'

Nicola was just sixteen when she joined the SNP. She promptly became an activist, giving up her regular Friday night ice-skating to become consumed by politics. Kay Ullrich, who was a candidate for the 1987 election, remembers a young Nicola knocking on her door and asking if she could help with her campaign. Ullrich lost, but says Nicola learned an important lesson from that experience: 'You can have a great campaign, you can work the hardest, you can win all the hustings meetings, you can have the best candidate, but unless you've got that swing, you ain't got a thing. She learned that very early on.'

In the autumn of 1988 Nicola arrived at Glasgow University to read Law. She took part in debates organised by the Glasgow University Scottish Nationalist Association and one of her fellow students recalls a determination rather than a natural talent: 'She'd turn up every week, and every week she was utterly rubbish . . . But she'd come back, again and again, trying to get it right, determined to figure out how she could get better.'

In 1992 she graduated with an upper second, narrowly missing out on a first. She puts it down to spending more time in politics than on the law, but she practised as a solicitor throughout the 1990s. After a couple of attempts to be elected, she finally became MSP for Glasgow in 1999 as a result of the proportional representation list. She had also been education spokesman for the SNP's Shadow Cabinet and her biography on the SNP website says, 'She has often commented that but for free tuition she would never have been able to further her education. For this reason she has resolved that for as long as she is in office the SNP will never reintroduce fees.'

In the 2004 election, where she failed to win the Govan seat, Nicola was thrown into a working relationship with her campaigns director, Peter Murrell, the SNP's Chief Executive. They married in 2010 and have no children. Quite rightly, when asked on *ITV Tonight* in 2015 whether she planned to have children, she shot back with her own query about whether the same question would have been asked of a childless male politician like Alex Salmond.

Throughout the 2000s she was given significant jobs in the shadow cabinet, including Health and Justice. In 2004 she became deputy leader of the SNP, and in 2007 she captured Govan at her fourth attempt. If Scotland had used only the first-past-the-post voting system it would have taken her eight attempts over fifteen years to win a majority in an election. She had made it so far because MSPs are elected partly by first-past-the-post and partly by a proportional representation method – the Additional Member System, which gives two votes to each elector. The SNP in 2007 became the largest party in the Parliament and began to rule as a minority government. Alex Salmond was First Minister and Nicola his deputy – the position she held until November 2014 when she became First Minister.

For her it's been a direct trajectory from the age of sixteen, putting in hard work to improve her public speaking and sharpening her personal presentation for the inevitable endless appearances on television and in the papers. She handles herself brilliantly in public, throwing off comments about her clothes, her weight and her nicknames – 'nippy sweetie' and 'able yin' – with a hint of contempt that such terms should be applied because she's a woman.

Nicola has not yet, though, achieved her aim: the independence of Scotland. After the pro-independence side lost the referendum, but did so spectacularly well in the general election of 2015, she was vague about the possible timing of a second referendum, telling the *Sunday Herald*, 'Our manifesto will set out what we think about the circumstances in which, and the possible timescales in which, a second referendum might be appropriate.'

The result of Britain's EU referendum on 23 June 2016 gave more impetus to her determination for Scottish independence. People throughout the United Kingdom had been asked 'Should the UK remain a member of the EU or leave the EU?' Nationally

51.89% voted to leave and 48.11% voted to remain, but Scotland voted in favour of remaining in the European Union and there was immediate discussion of the constitutional questions. Could Scotland block the UK's exit or would a hasty move towards independence through a second referendum be required?

From that point matters moved on apace. The then Prime Minister, David Cameron, resigned. Theresa May won the contest for leadership of the Conservative party, becoming Britain's second female Prime Minister on 13 July. She demonstrated a fierce determination to negotiate Britain's exit from the EU, known as Brexit, as quickly as possible and made it clear from the outset that she was keen that the UK should appear united. She made an early commitment to maintaining the union. Sturgeon is equally determined that Scotland should again seek independence and be free to remain a member of the European Union.

There appears to be no love lost between two of the most powerful politicians in western Europe. In March 2017 Sturgeon sought the approval of the Scottish Parliament to request the Prime Minister's permission for a second Scottish Independence Referendum to be held in Spring 2019, when Britain is expected to leave the EU. Her parliament agreed. May's response was that 'this is not the time for such a discussion'.

The meeting between the two women on 28 March 2017 was decidedly frosty. No progress was made that might have satisfied Sturgeon's aspirations, but perhaps the most depressing aspect of their encounter was a photograph of the two of them which was widely distributed in the press. Both wore shortish skirts, tights and court shoes. The headlines screamed 'Legsit'. A Prime Minister and a First Minister were judged on their legs rather than their policies. There's still a long way for women to go to be taken entirely seriously.

Sturgeon's fearless single-mindedness has never been more apparent than in her dealings with the new President of the United

States, Donald Trump. During his period as a candidate she had him stripped of his title of business ambassador for the Scottish government in the wake of his call for Muslims to be banned from entry into the US. When he won the election in November 2016 she sent her congratulations, but said to the Scottish Parliament that she stood by her criticism of him because many of his comments during the campaign had been 'deeply abhorrent'.

'I never want to be, I am not prepared to be,' she said, 'a politician that maintains diplomatic silence in the face of attitudes of racism, sexism, misogyny or intolerance of any kind. I think it is important today that, firstly, I hope that President-elect Trump turns out to be a President very different to the kind of candidate he was and reaches out to those who felt vilified by his campaign.'

No danger then of Ms Sturgeon mincing her words. Thus far, as regards her desire for Scottish Independence, it's a case of wait and see, but the impact of Nicola Sturgeon on the history of Great Britain, if her mother's prediction that Nicola will always achieve what she wants to achieve is correct, will be profound. The *Daily Mail*'s 'most dangerous woman in Britain' may well take Scotland away.

# AFTERWORD

S o, there they are. The twenty-one women who, across the
centuries, have defied conventional expectations of a
woman's lot in life and slowly, slowly changed Britain's
gender landscape for us. And we are lucky to live in the country
they helped to create.

We are no longer forced into marriages by domineering fathers
and, if we are, there's a law to protect us. We don't have to give
birth to babies we can't care for. We have access to free contraception, abortion is legal and we can choose the kind of sex life
we want to engage in, whether straight or gay, both or neither.

We can wear pretty much what we want and when a company
like PricewaterhouseCoopers insists that a young woman, Nicola
Thorp, must wear high heels for work there's a national outcry,
asking why a woman can't wear comfy flats. No one dictates what
kind of shoes a man should go out in.

We have an equal right to free schooling, and universities take
the brightest and the best, regardless of gender. We are fully
recognised as citizens of Britain, but I do sometimes wish women
would be more appreciative of the vote that our predecessors

suffered beatings and imprisonment to win for us. It's an insult to them all that so many of us can't be bothered to make the effort to go to the polling station. If we fail to take a full part in the democratic process, we are simply allowing this country in which we live to continue to be man-made.

And let's not assume that we can be complacent and think that everything has now been fixed. Laws are all fine and dandy, but they don't change the prejudice that persists. There were 191 female MPs elected to Parliament at the last election in 2015 – a mere twenty-nine per cent. It's a record high, but it's a long way from fifty-fifty representation. Equal pay has still not been achieved. Quite where the pay gap stands at the moment is unclear. The Fawcett Society has it at 13.9% based on the average wage for full-time workers. The Office for National Statistics says 'the pay gap narrowed to 9.4% for full-time employees in 2015', but an article in the *Guardian* newspaper in March 2016 places it at '24% in average full-time salaries between men and women'. Whatever the answer, the pay gap exists and it's significant.

Women make up eighty per cent of workers in the low-paid care and leisure sectors. Only ten per cent of the better paid skilled tradespeople are female. Around 54,000 women are forced to leave their jobs every year because they are pregnant, even though it's against the law to discriminate against a woman who's having a baby. At the very top there are fewer women leading FTSE firms than men called John.

Among the seven demands of the Women's Liberation Movement, made in 1971, were free twenty-four-hour nurseries, and financial and legal independence. Reliable affordable childcare has never been taken up by any government, and it's impossible to have financial independence if you can't hold down a job or have to work part time because you can't afford to pay the exorbitant rates demanded by childcare providers.

The seventh demand of the movement, laid down at the National Women's Liberation Conference in 1978, was 'Freedom from intimidation by threat or use of violence or sexual coercion, regardless of marital status, and an end to all laws, assumptions and institutions which perpetuate male dominance and men's aggression towards women.'

The laws are in place. It's illegal to rape, sexually assault, coerce, intimidate, stalk or abuse online. But we know that approximately 85,000 women and 12,000 men are raped every year in England and Wales with only 5.7% of reported rape cases leading to a conviction of the perpetrator. Domestic violence is rife, with the Office for National Statistics showing that 1.4 million women suffered abuse in the home between 2013 and 2014, and two women every week are murdered by a current or former partner. In early summer of 2016 a coalition of female politicians announced their determination to end misogynist bullying online. Extreme pornography is everywhere on the internet.

As far as women and sport are concerned, Nicola Sturgeon, disgusted as she was, and despite all the woman power she's brought to Scotland, couldn't stop the Muirfield Golf Club voting in 2016 to prevent women becoming members or prevent a veteran golf commentator, Peter Alliss, suggesting that women who wanted to play at the club should marry a member.

There is still a long way to go. No era has been as misnamed as the one that began to be described in the late 1980s as post-feminist. Feminism is as necessary now as it was for every woman in this book. And what we must be wary of is sitting pretty on our laurels believing the battle for equality is won and we can all ease up.

It's just over twenty-five years since I first read Margaret Atwood's *The Handmaid's Tale*. It's the story of a country taken over by a far-right religious movement where women are made to be wives or handmaidens – a solution to a catastrophic decline in fertility. Men are the commanders in public and in the home. They have all the power, and breeding takes place when the handmaiden is at the height of her fertile cycle. The commander mounts her while the (infertile) wife looks on. That was shocking enough, but I remember clearly that moment when Offred, the central character, goes to use her credit card and is told no, that she has no money in the bank because women are no longer allowed to have any independent means. For a moment I thought, 'Come on Margaret, interesting dystopian piece of work, but it could never happen.'

And then it did. It happened in Afghanistan, a country where, at the same time as I was wearing short skirts and going to university, Afghani women were enjoying the same freedoms. Then the Taliban took power and a woman was not allowed to go out without a male companion, had to be covered from head to toe, and was not allowed any kind of job. In the Middle East the treatment of women by similarly extreme groups of Islamic fundamentalists such as so-called Islamic State, or Daesh, is beyond medieval.

We should never assume that rights once won are written in stone and can't be taken away. We must not relax our vigilance. It is vital that the rights won thus far remain in place for the girls and women who follow us. We all, men and women, have to support them in their struggles to make things even better until complete equality is achieved. My twenty-one Great Britons never gave up, and neither must we.

# ACKNOWLEDGEMENTS

Thank you to Dr Anna Whitelock and Eleanor Garland for their help with my research; my editor Sam Carter at Oneworld and my agent Barbara Levy for their guidance and support in making this book a reality; Tamsin Shelton for making sure I don't fall into the journalist's trap of caring more about a good story than the facts, Peter Locke for his beautiful illustrations of these inspiring women, and my neighbours Barbara and Chris for all of their dog-walking support.

# ABOUT THE AUTHOR

Jenni Murray is a journalist and broadcaster who has presented BBC Radio 4's *Woman's Hour* since 1987. She regularly contributes to various newspapers and magazines, and is the author of several books, including *Memoirs of a Not So Dutiful Daughter*. She lives in London and the Peak District.